# *Receiving* Mantles

## FROM THE

## COURTS OF HEAVEN

# Destiny Image Books by Robert Henderson

*365 Prayers and Activations for Entering the Courts of Heaven*

*Unlocking Wealth from the Courts of Heaven*

*Resetting Economies from the Courts of Heaven*
(mini-book)

*Breaking the Stronghold of Iniquity*
(with Bill Dennington)

*Petitioning the Courts of Heaven During Times of Crisis*
(mini-book)

*Operating in the Courts of Heaven*

*Show Us Your Glory*

*Praying for the Prophetic Destiny of the United States and the Presidency of Donald J. Trump from the Courts of Heaven*

*Father, Friend, and Judge*

*Issuing Divine Restraining Orders from Courts of Heaven*
(with Dr. Francis Myles)

*Redeeming Your Bloodline*
(with Hrvoje Sirovina)

*The Cloud of Witnesses in the Courts of Heaven*

*Prayers and Declarations that Open the Courts of Heaven*

*Receiving Healing from the Courts of Heaven, Curriculum*

*Accessing the Courts of Heaven*

*Unlocking Destinies from the Courts of Heaven, Curriculum*

*Receiving Generational Blessings from the Courts of Heaven*

# *Receiving* Mantles

## FROM THE
## COURTS OF HEAVEN

Supernatural Empowerment to
Fulfill the Call of God on Your Life

## ROBERT
## HENDERSON

Please note that Destiny Image's publishing style capitalizes certain pronouns that refer to the Father, Son, and Holy Spirit, and may differ from some publishers' styles. Take note that the name satan and related names are not capitalized. We choose not to acknowledge him, even to the point of violating grammatical rules.

DESTINY IMAGE® PUBLISHERS, INC.
P.O. Box 310, Shippensburg, PA 17257-0310
*"Promoting Inspired Lives."*

This book and all other Destiny Image and Destiny Image Fiction books are available at Christian bookstores and distributors worldwide.

For more information on foreign distributors, call 717-532-3040.

Reach us on the Internet: www.destinyimage.com.

ISBN 13 TP: 978-0-7684-6330-9

ISBN 13 eBook: 978-0-7684-6331-6

ISBN 13 HC: 978-0-7684-6333-0

ISBN 13 LP: 978-0-7684-6332-3

For Worldwide Distribution, Printed in the U.S.A.

1 2 3 4 5 6 7 8 / 26 25 24 23 22

# CONTENTS

# INTRODUCTION

What many people do not know about me is that my life didn't begin with the Courts of Heaven teaching. This message the Lord gave me to carry and impregnate the Body of Christ with is a huge part of who I am. However, from my earliest memory I have had a passion for the power and glory of the Lord. I love His presence and the anointing. I have sought the Lord and desired to witness His majesty displayed upon people's lives. As I stepped away from a more pastoral function and into an itinerant role, I thought that I would be a healing revivalist. This is what my passion was and what I thought I would do. This was the way I was primarily functioning at this time. However, as I started to travel it became clear that I was going to manifest a much more apostolic dimension. I began to challenge the Body of Christ to move out of a pastoral expression and into an apostolic one. As a result of this, I dove-tailed into the Courts of Heaven teaching as this revelation grabbed hold. I have written many books on the Courts of Heaven and continue to write them. As I said, it is a primary piece of who I am and what I do. It is an assignment from the Lord for my life.

Coupled with this, a dear prophetic friend suddenly communicated with me that he had a dream about me. I read the dream he sent me and was immediately intrigued by it. The dream was quite specific and detailed. I would like to relate this dream. I will then share understanding the Lord has given concerning it. These are the words of my friend Prophet Greg Hood:

> The dream opened with you and me sitting in this old style diner eating breakfast. I can see the table and the plates on it. There was an old style jukebox there—the kind that hung at the table wall.
>
> As we ate, we were talking about mantles. I was sharing with you that my grandfather and my father had passed away and that in a dream, Holy Spirit had mantled me with their mantle. As I was sharing this with you, a man walked up to our table. He was the manager of this diner. He said to us, "Gentlemen, I have a dilemma that I know you will help me with." He went on to say,

"Look over in the corner at that coatrack. There are so many coats that have been left here, and I can't get them to their rightful owners. These are not the old owners but the new ones." He said, "Come with me." We got up from the table and followed him out the front door.

As we exited the diner with this man, we were instantly in heaven. This man was actually an angel. He walked us through a portion of a building there in heaven that led us to a closet. This closet was the size of a football field. It was full of so many coats, robes, capes, suit coats, and jackets. These coats had all types of logos on them and were every color and size you could imagine. They were also arranged according to the seven gates/mountains of influence. He said to us, "Each coat has on its left lapel a dial." It had numbers on them that went from one to one hundred. These gauges determine at what power level the mantle operates. The coats also had names written in the collar of each one. Some had many names and some only a few names and some only one name. As he was speaking to us, another angel walked up to him and handed him a scroll. He opened the scroll and read it to himself. He then handed it to me and he said, "Greg, declare this Word of the Lord over Robert." He then said to you, "Robert, as he does, you're going to help me empty out this warehouse of mantles." You and I both noticed his words. He used the word *mantles*, not *coats*.

I then took the open scroll and began to declare it over you. When I looked at you, I saw you were dressed like a tailor with a measuring tape in your hand. I declared, "You, Robert Henderson, have been assigned by the Father to bring His people into their mantles. You and your company of tailors will measure and fit from My closet mantles that have been laid down and never picked up. You will find many who are wandering through life without meaning and purpose. You and your company of tailors will fit them. You will write again of My Courts and how mantles are released from there." The Lord says over you, "This is the great activation and release of My people in the nation of the United States of America. There are some who will find their portion and many who will discover their double portion." After declaring over you, I rolled up the scroll and placed it in the right inside pocket of your coat. I then began to prophesy over you that Holy Spirit was cutting four new highways into Waco and the nation, and nations would began to pour into Waco to get their mantle. There will be those from every walk of life pouring into your place in Waco to find their mantle. Leaders of nations will come and receive mantles and take them back to cities, regions, and the nations. We then turned and walked from the warehouse with the angel. As we came to the door, he handed you a key and said to you, "Robert, you have been given full access to this closet at any time. Pull from it! Bring people to it. This is the time for the nation to be awakened."

In the dream, instantly we were back in the diner. The manager said to us, "Don't forget those on the coat rack. They are fresh and ready to wear." Your son Adam came through the door with a sound system, a pulpit, and your Bible. Your other children followed him with other equipment. They set it up beside the coat rack. There was a line of people forming at the door. You and I noticed that the diner was now three to four

> times larger than it was in the beginning of the dream.

This dream has many intriguing ideas associated with it. The first thing that should be known is that I have had for many years an anointing to impart anointing to others. In November of 1999 I had a dream where I went to a very prominent healing evangelist. He agreed to come to where I was. In this dream, he also sat me down with his team who taught me how to lead a healing service. As I awakened from the dream, I felt the Lord say to me that this man represented the healing anointing. If I would *go after* it, I could have it.

So many people do not understand this. You have to contend for and go after what even God has called you to. One cannot be passive or complacent in the matter. What God has is only for the hungry and thirsty. I also knew from this dream that I was going to be instructed in how to function in this anointing that I was to receive. I remember in January of 2000 the Lord told me to begin to teach on Jesus' healing ministry. I want to say here that when I say the *Lord told me,* I say it with fear and trembling. I don't always hear the Lord this clearly. However, in these instances I am describing, the Lord's voice seemed to be very real and close. As I began to teach on Jesus' healing ministry in an effort to *go after* the healing anointing, healings began to happen. Significant things such as broken bones being instantly mended occurred. Birth deformities were suddenly healed. Deaf ears began to open. Many other things were happening. It was as if the Lord was honoring our very childlike faith and even immature efforts to obey Him. We began to see healings, miracles, and the like on a regular basis.

A few months later, the healing evangelist I saw in my dream was scheduled to be in the Dallas/Fort Worth area. I received an invitation to attend a pastors' planning session connected to the healing crusade that would be held in that area. At the time of the meeting I was very busy. I remember considering not attending. It was an hour and a half drive away from me, and I thought, *What good would it do?* Only because of my dream of *going after* the healing anointing and being taught how to lead a healing service did I reluctantly go. I walked into the room filled with pastors and sat at the very back table next to the door, intending to make a quick exit as soon as I could.

As I was sitting there not knowing anyone, one of the men hosting this meeting came and sat down at the table. We began to converse. For whatever reason, I told him the dream I had about going to the healing evangelist (his boss). I had no idea who he was or what he did for the ministry. I didn't know that one of his jobs was determining who could sit on the platform during the crusades. As soon as the meeting was over, I left and drove back home. By the time I arrived at the office, the ministry of the healing evangelist had already called and asked if I would like to sit on the platform during the crusade. Of course my answer was a resounding "Yes." Little did I know that my life was about to change forever!

As the day came for the crusade, I was in prayer that morning. As I prayed, I heard the Lord say, *"Today I give you an endowment."* *Endowment* is not a word I use on a regular basis. An *endowment* is "an income or form of property given or bequeathed to someone." It can also mean "resources supplied until an assignment is accomplished." I believed and realized that God had appointed me to be anointed or *mantled* for an assignment. I went to the crusade with a great expectation in my heart. As the meeting progressed, there was a time when the healing evangelist began to pray for the pastors. As I came and stood before him, as hundreds and thousands did that day, a tremendous power of the Lord was imparted to me. I was touched in an amazing way as the Spirit of the Lord came on my life. Making a long story short, I returned to the place of ministry I had and began to see greater and more miracles, but also the ability to impart mantles to others. The *endowment* that the Lord spoke to me about was a mantle that I was to carry. This mantle would involve signs, wonders, and miracles. It would also empower me in my apostolic call. This would allow me to *impart* mantles to other people as well.

Several years later when my prophet friend Greg Hood had this dream, it made perfect sense. Even though I have imparted mantles to many others, I knew it was the season/convergence time for what I had received to be massively imparted.

In the dream about mantles I think it is significant that we were sitting in a diner from the past. As much as I appreciate any *new thing* the Lord is doing, there is something about the power that comes from what might be called "old school." A life of consecration, seeking God, and separation to the Lord cannot have a substitute. If we are to see the glory of God and carry mantles from Him, there is a cost associated. We must fall desperately in love with Him and allow this to radically affect our life. As we do, we will qualify to carry the mantles of the Lord ordained for us.

The mantles that were stored in heavenly places were mantles that were not being used. I believe this is for two reasons. One is people don't know they are available. They haven't been taught. They know little or nothing about the power and anointing of the Spirit of God. Second, few are willing to pay the price I have spoken of previously. There is a lifestyle adjustment required to carry the mantles of the Lord. Ephesians 4:1 exhorts us to walk in a worthy way.

> *I, therefore, the prisoner of the Lord, beseech you to walk worthy of the calling with which you were called.*

Paul declared himself to be the prisoner of the Lord. This means his life was no longer his. He didn't have the right to choose his own ways, but was at the discretion of the One who owned him. This must become our mantra as well. We must with great joy give ourselves to Him for His purposes. We are not our own; we are His! Once this is done, it will propel us into a worthy walk to qualify us to carry the mantling of the Lord. There are mantles in the heavenly realm waiting to be dispensed and dispersed into our lives. May we qualify as those who can righteously steward these for the glory and purpose of the Lord.

The dream also reveals that the names of those who previously carried the mantles were written in the collars. Some had many names, some had a few and others only had one. There are mantles and anointings given on the basis of the call of God. The Bible says of Jesus that He was anointed and was mantled by the Father in an unusual way. He had an anointing *above* His brothers. Hebrews 1:8-9 tells us that Jesus qualified as the Son for a great anointing.

*But to the Son He says:*

*"Your throne, O God, is forever and ever;*

*A scepter of righteousness is the scepter of Your kingdom.*

*You have loved righteousness and hated lawlessness;*

*Therefore God, Your God, has anointed You*

*With the oil of gladness more than Your companions."*

Jesus was greatly anointed with the oil of gladness. The anointing He carried was full of joy and happiness. I believe He imparted this wherever He went. Notice this mantle/anointing was a result of loving righteousness and hating lawlessness. If we are to carry the unusual anointings, it will require us to have His nature. Notice that we are to *love,* then we can *hate.* I remember a great man of God many years ago saying, *"It is very dangerous to hate more than you love."* What a statement. Any hatred we have for lawlessness and iniquity must flow from a love and passion for righteousness. Only the Lord can put this in us by His nature. His nature causes us to love what I used to hate and hate what I used to love. This is the result of being born again. When we were born again, the Father's seed and nature was placed in us. Second Peter 1:4 speaks of this divine nature.

*By which have been given to us exceedingly great and precious promises, that through these you may be partakers of the divine nature, having escaped the corruption that is in the world through lust.*

This divine nature that we have become partakers of causes us to escape the corruption in this world. This corruption is a result of a life driven by lust. When we are granted His nature, we begin to love righteousness and hate iniquity. The more we let this be formed in us, the more we qualify for these special mantles that only a few can carry—or maybe even one has carried. May we be anointed and mantled with the anointing above our brothers. Not so we can have a superior attitude, but so we can be used to accomplish things for the kingdom that are necessary. May we be of that usefulness to the Lord.

Notice that the dream also spoke of tailors who would be used to fit people with their mantles. I believe these are people joined to me in ministry who can get people ready for the mantles they are called to carry. The mantles waiting to be dispersed don't change. They are heavenly and they are divine. When we speak of something being *tailored,* we are speaking of the one called to carry the mantle. In other words, the tailoring is not done on the mantle; it is done on the person called to carry it. We must be changed, altered, and prepared to fit the mantle, not the mantle to fit us. This is why so often mantles are not given and received. We want the mantle to change to fit us, when it is we who must be changed to fit the mantle. As the fivefold ministry gifts, we must prepare the people to receive, carry, and function in their mantle from heaven. Ephesians 4:11-13 tells us of the effect of these ministry gifts on our lives.

> *And He Himself gave some to be apostles, some prophets, some evangelists, and some pastors and teachers, for the equipping of the saints for the work of ministry, for the edifying of the body of Christ, till we all come to the unity of the faith and of the knowledge of the Son of God, to a perfect man, to the measure of the stature of the fullness of Christ.* We are all to be equipped, aligned, and brought into a demonstration of Jesus' stature. This means we grow up and change. We come into realms of maturity. This allows us to be fitted with the mantle of the Lord. God changes our character to fit the anointing we are called to carry. He uses the *tailors* to do this in our lives.

These mantles also had *dials* on them that determined the level of power they would operate at. The level of power is connected to the call and assignment that has be given. I think about the servants who were trusted with their master's goods in Matthew 25:15. The master gave them currency to trade with and make increase. He trusted them on the basis of their *ability*.

> *And to one he gave five talents, to another two, and to another one, to each according to his own ability; and immediately he went on a journey.*

The number of talents trusted to each servant was based on their *ability*. The word *ability* is the Greek word *dunamis*. It means *power*. It normally speaks of the anointing one carries. If this is true, then the amount of currency given was based on the level of power that each one had. I am citing this to point out that the mantle we carry and the power level of it can determine what we have been given authority over. The dial on the lapel of the mantle determined the level of power and, therefore, the level of responsibility entrusted. The truth is that if we are faithful, we can be entrusted with more. If we use the level of power we are given to get our assignment accomplished, we will be given more. We are told that if we are faithful and use what we have, more will be entrusted. Matthew 25:29 lets us know that when we use the power level we have faithfully, it will lead to abundance and much more.

*For to everyone who has, more will be given, and
he will have abundance; but from him who does
not have, even what he has will be taken away.*

If we don't use the power level we have, then we
can lose even what has been given to us. We cannot
allow our perceived smallness of power to cause us to
not be faithful. We must take what we have, not compare it to others, and move in wise stewardship. We
are promised increase as we do.

It is the passion of the Lord to impart mantles to us
to fulfill our call. However, the devil wants to resist
this. It is my opinion that one of the reasons we lack
mantles to accomplish the task is the devil's legal case
against us. If we can step into the Courts of Heaven
and remove these claims, we can position ourselves
for our assigned mantles. We can get ready to receive
them and the empowerment they bring. The result will
be His kingdom will done and our lives fulfilled.

# CHAPTER 1

# MANTLES AND
# THE COURTS OF HEAVEN

As with almost any other kingdom realm, the devil will seek to resist you from the mantling of God. The devil is greatly afraid of those who carry the anointing of the Lord. Isaiah 10:27 shows us the power of one anointed of God.

> *It shall come to pass in that day*
> *That his burden will be taken away from your shoulder,*
> *And his yoke from your neck,*
> *And the yoke will be destroyed because of the anointing oil.*

The anointing oil promises to destroy the yokes. Yokes are used to control. This is why farmers and others place yokes on animals. They can be directed and controlled no matter how strong and huge they are. The yoke goes on the neck and therefore controls the head. If you can control the head, you can determine the direction taken no matter the power of an animal. This means that yokes in the spiritual realm are designed to control thinking and mindsets.

When someone has a yoke on them, their minds are being directed. If the mind and thinking is controlled, then the whole person is controlled. Notice, however, that it is the anointing oil that destroys the yoke. That which is exercising control over the mindsets of people is broken off. This includes self-image issues, mindsets, philosophies, and ideologies. These are powerful demonic things that control people and even groups of people. We see this in Second Corinthians 10:4-6.

> For the weapons of our warfare are not carnal but mighty in God for pulling down strongholds, casting down arguments and every high thing that exalts itself against the knowledge of God, bringing every thought into captivity to the obedience of Christ, and being ready to punish all disobedience when your obedience is fulfilled.

Strongholds, arguments, high things against the knowledge of God, and unruly thoughts are all dealing with the mindset of people. Paul declared that there were weapons to destroy these things that dominate the thoughts of people. We know that if the thoughts of people are controlled, their lives are controlled. The often quoted Proverbs 23:7 says our lives are a result of our thinking process.

*For as he thinks in his heart, so is he.*

When we liberate the thinking, we change the lives of people completely. At least one of the weapons that destroy these yokes is the anointing. It would stand to reason that the devil desires to stop us from being anointed/mantled. This would prohibit people's lives from being set free.

Before we go into the Courts of Heaven and discuss how to secure mantles from that realm, we need to understand this word *anointing*. Again, as a reminder, it is the *anointing oil* that destroys the yokes. The word *anointing* is the Hebrew word *shenen*. It means "grease, especially something liquid." Grease is the result of something being heated up until the oil in it is extracted. One of the most common pictures of this is bacon. When bacon is fried, great amounts of grease are forced from it. The result is quite a bit of liquid that is left over after the intense heating of this bacon.

The same is true for our lives. The kind of anointing that destroys yokes is this anointing. It is the result of navigating through intense times when the heat of life extracts the anointing of God. When we walk through these times and respond correctly, the mantles of God can be ours. Otherwise, the devil will use our disobedience in these times against us. Just because we go through difficult times doesn't mean it will result in a greater anointing. Only when we humble ourselves in these times will this be the result. We can qualify for the mantles of God. Otherwise, we have just gone through a hard time for nothing.

Paul spoke of this in Second Corinthians 1:3-6. He talked of the comfort they received from the Lord that actually empowered them to comfort others.

> *Blessed be the God and Father of our Lord Jesus Christ, the Father of mercies and God of all comfort, who comforts us in all our tribulation, that we may be able to comfort those who are in any trouble, with the comfort with which we ourselves are comforted by God. For as the sufferings of Christ abound in us, so our consolation also abounds through Christ. Now if we are afflicted, it is for your consolation and salvation, which is effective for enduring the same sufferings which we also suffer. Or if we are comforted, it is for your consolation and salvation.*

Notice that the power to comfort came from the comfort they received directly from God. In their tribulation, they were able to find the love and care of the

Lord. This clearly produced an anointing in their life to give to others. This is a picture of the anointing of God coming on their life because of *how* they walked through difficulty. In times of testing we either qualify for the greater anointing or mantle, or we become disqualified. Not everyone gets through places of difficulty successfully. They end up divorced, going into rebellion, forsaking the Lord, and other forms of disobedience. They don't realize that choices in these moments of hardship are speaking on their behalf in the Courts of Heaven. However, wrong choices in these times allow the devil the right to make cases to deny them the mantling of the Lord. From my perspective, the devil is seeking to find a case against us to stop us from these greater realms.

Allow me to explain how this works in the Courts of Heaven. In Daniel 7:9-10 we see the Courts of Heaven being revealed.

> *I watched till thrones were put in place,*
> *And the Ancient of Days was seated;*
> *His garment was white as snow,*
> *And the hair of His head was like pure wool.*
> *His throne was a fiery flame,*
> *Its wheels a burning fire;*
> *A fiery stream issued*

*And came forth from before Him.*

*A thousand thousands ministered to Him;*

*Ten thousand times ten thousand stood before Him.*

*The court was seated,*

*And the books were opened.*

Daniel as a seer was seeing into the unseen realm of the spirit. This is why he says, *I watched.* He sees multiple thrones with the Throne of God set in place. It speaks of the fiery stream that came forth from His Throne as the *Ancient of Days.* This title speaks of the absolute preeminence of who God is. He was and is and is to come. He is the God of all wisdom and knowledge. Therefore, His judgments are always right and just! I believe the fiery stream is the judgment of the Lord coming from His Throne. Psalm 97:3 tells us that this fiery stream consumes all of the enemies of God.

*A fire goes before Him,*

*And burns up His enemies round about.*

His enemies are anything or anyone who opposes His will from being done in the earth. There are legal renderings from the Throne of God that cause these enemies to be removed. Their legal right of operation is revoked. As we will see, we are a part of presenting cases in these Courts that allow this to occur. This is why Jesus placed prayer in a judicial setting in Luke 18:1-8. He spoke of a widow with no power or might. However, she was successful in getting a verdict from an unjust judge.

> *Then He spoke a parable to them, that men always ought to pray and not lose heart, saying: "There was in a certain city a judge who did not fear God nor regard man. Now there was a widow in that city; and she came to him, saying, 'Get justice for me from my adversary.' And he would not for a while; but afterward he said within himself, 'Though I do not fear God nor regard man, yet because this widow troubles me I will avenge her, lest by her continual coming she weary me.'" Then the Lord said, "Hear what the unjust judge said. And shall God not avenge His own elect who cry out day and night to Him, though He bears long with them? I tell you that He will avenge them speedily. Nevertheless, when the Son of Man comes, will He really find faith on the earth?"*

There is a principle lesson from this teaching on prayer that Jesus gave. It is, if this widow could get a verdict/decision from an unjust judge, how much more can we get a verdict and answer from God, the

Judge of all? We too have the right to come and stand in the Courts of Heaven and petition Him as our Judge.

Let me point out three things about the Courts of Heaven from Jesus' teaching. First, the widow had an adversary. This is the Greek word *antidikos*. This word literally means "one who brings a lawsuit, our legal opponent." We must recognize that satan is our legal opponent and adversary. First Peter 5:8 settles this.

> *Be sober, be vigilant; because your adversary the devil walks about like a roaring lion, seeking whom he may devour.*

This word *adversary* is the same word, *antidikos*. Notice that the devil as our legal opponent is looking to devour us. He wants to destroy our live, future, faith, and family. He is looking for a legal right to devour us as our legal opponent who brings cases against us. We are told we must be on guard and diligent to protect ourselves against this. The word *antidikos* comes from two Greek words, *anti* and *dikos*. *Anti* means to be "against or instead of." *Dikos* means "rights." The purpose of the devil's lawsuit against us is to *deny us what is rightfully ours*. We know that we have covenant with God through the blood and body of Jesus. In this covenant is everything that pertains to life and godliness. This is according to Second Peter 1:3.

*As His divine power has given to us all things that pertain to life and godliness, through the knowledge of Him who called us by glory and virtue.*

We have salvation, healing, life, forgiveness, prosperity, and everything else that bring happiness and joy to us. This has been granted to us by the sacrifice of Jesus. It is rightfully ours by virtue of who Jesus is and what He has done. However, the devil, our antidikos/adversary, has cases against us. These cases are denying us what is rightfully ours. We must know how to go into the Courts of Heaven and secure all that belongs to us. Through all that Jesus has done, we can answer any and every case and secure our inheritance in God!

A second thing we can realize is that the Courts of Heaven are for the *elect*. This is what Jesus said was one of the main lessons to this story. He said if this widow could get a verdict from the unjust judge, *how much more will God avenge His own elect!* I have had people say they were afraid to approach God as Judge. This is because they don't realize the Court of Heaven is the place where the elect's cause against the devil is heard. In this place, the devil's right that is being claimed is revoked. The Court of Heaven is for the elect and chosen of God. We don't have to fear this place. Romans

8:33 tells us that as the elect of God, no charge against us can stick.

> *Who shall bring a charge against God's elect? It*
> *is God who justifies.*

This is from a legal perspective. It is impossible for the devil to bring a case against us that can be effective. If we know how to take advantage of the Courts of Heaven, we will always be avenged and vindicated before the Lord. We as the *elect* have a status and place before His Courts that allow our justification because of what Jesus has done for us. Peter spoke of this place of His elect as well. First Peter 1:1-2 shows Peter writing to those who are dispersed and scattered. He declares that because of the foreknowledge of God, we are His elect.

> *Peter, an apostle of Jesus Christ,*
>
> *To the pilgrims of the Dispersion in Pontus,*
> *Galatia, Cappadocia, Asia, and Bithynia, elect*
> *according to the foreknowledge of God the Father,*
> *in sanctification of the Spirit, for obedience and*
> *sprinkling of the blood of Jesus Christ:*
>
> *Grace to you and peace be multiplied.*

Notice that God from His foreknowledge granted us a position before Him as His elect. This was before we did anything good or bad. My election is based on Jesus' blood, the Holy Spirit's work, and God's heart toward me. You and I have the status as the elect of God before His Courts. As with the widow in Jesus' teaching, the Courts of Heaven are the place where our adversary is judged. We take him to Court even as the widow did her opponent.

The third thing that stands out in Jesus' teaching is His remark about the story He told. He said, *"God will avenge quickly those who cry out day and night to Him."* This phrase used to confuse me. It appeared paradoxical. He says God would do something *quick,* yet the term *day and night* spoke of long, enduring praying. Then I felt the Lord spoke to me and unveiled what was being communicated. When we have cried out to the Lord in ongoing, persistent prayer, this develops a history with God. This grants us a status and place of influence before Him. Therefore, when we step into His Courts from this history, we are heard. Our case is esteemed and we are avenged against our adversary.

This was my experience as I began to enter the Courts of Heaven. I saw, and still see today, great and even immediate breakthroughs that come as I function in the Courts of Heaven. oI asked someone who, at that time, had much more experience in functioning in the Courts of Heaven why this was. The response surprised me. They said my experience of breakthrough was much quicker because I had "done the work." I then began to think about how I had sought the face of God daily for 30-plus years. I have endeavored to be a man of prayer who seeks His face. The promise of God's Word in Hebrews 11:6 is that He will reward those who seek Him.

> But without faith it is impossible to please Him, for he who comes to God must believe that He is, and that He is a rewarder of those who diligently seek Him.

Real faith will seek Him. There will be set aside times on a regular schedule when we approach Him and His Throne. This gained me a status before the Courts. As a result of my diligent seeking of Him, the moment I stepped into the Courts of Heaven, massive breakthrough came! You do not have to pray for 30 years before this happens for you. However, I would encourage the development of a life of prayer before the Lord. This will give you a history with the Lord. It will result in answers coming quickly, even as Jesus promised.

These three things are of great advantage as we come before the Courts of Heaven. We must recognize the devil is your legal opponent. Anything he seeks to do will be from a legal perspective. Second, we are the elect of God. We have already been granted a position before the Courts of Heaven that will allow us to over-come. May we believe this place we have been given and function in it with great boldness. Third, God will reward from His Courts those who have and continue to diligently seek Him. This gives us status with the Courts because we have been those who have sought Him. We can get breakthroughs quickly.

In regard to *receiving mantles* from the Courts of Heaven, we must learn how to take these principles and operate in them. We can renounce any legal claims the devil is using to stop our mantling. Any case he is espousing against us we can see annulled. From our position as His elect and our heart to seek Him, we can petition the Courts to dismiss satan's cases. We can repent for any place we haven't been faithful in difficulty and hardship. We can ask for Jesus' blood to speak for us and silence the voices of the devil. Hebrews 12:24 tells us that Jesus' blood is testifying a much better thing than what Abel's blood said.

> *To Jesus the Mediator of the new covenant, and to the blood of sprinkling that speaks better things than that of Abel.*

Abel's blood caused the judgment of Cain to be set into place. Abel's blood cried for vengeance. However, Jesus' blood cries for forgiveness, mercy, and redemp-tion. Jesus' blood is used to silence every voice of the devil as our legal opponent. Any claim he is making that would be used to deny us our mantle can be silenced. Any place we faltered in the place of hardship, trial, and struggle, we can repent and ask for Jesus' blood to speak for us. His blood will secure for us redemption. His blood and its testimony for us will qualify us for the mantling of the Lord.

> As I come before Your Courts, Lord, let it be recorded that I desire to walk in a worthy manner before You. I ask, for any hardship I might have had to endure, that I would have grace to overcome. May the anointing oil be upon me as a result of that which I have endured by Your power and might.
>
> Let me be one, I pray, who has a status in Your Courts. Let me stand before You as the elect of God, chosen, and a special people before You. Allow me, Lord, to bring a case against my adversary who would seek to legally resist me. Let any effort that he might bring to deny me what is rightfully mine be revoked. I stand before You as one chosen by You because of the blood of Jesus.
>
> I also ask that my history with You might be regarded before this Court. I have been one who has sought You day and night.

Therefore, I ask that there would be a speedy acquittal of any charges the adversary would bring. Let me stand before You as one worthy to receive the mantling of the Lord for the call of God on my life. Allow anything that would hinder this to be removed and revoked I pray, in Jesus' Name. Amen!

CHAPTER 2

# HUNGER:
# KEY TO THE MANTLE

We cannot speak of the mantles of the Lord without talking about Elijah and Elisha. This is the predominant place where we see an impartation of the mantling of God. Elisha received from Elijah "his" mantle that came to him as he was translated away. Elisha's hunger, obedience, and pursuit allowed him to qualify for this transaction. In other words, there was nothing legal to resist Elisha from receiving the mantle and anointing. Elisha's capturing of this mantle was at least partially because his obedience was speaking for him in the Courts of Heaven. I would like to look at some of the things that qualified Elisha to receive and carry this mantle. Second Kings 2:1-15 gives us the story of the impartation of this mantle.

*And it came to pass, when the Lord was about to take up Elijah into heaven by a whirlwind, that*

*Elijah went with Elisha from Gilgal. Then Elijah said to Elisha, "Stay here, please, for the Lord has sent me on to Bethel."*

*But Elisha said, "As the Lord lives, and as your soul lives, I will not leave you!" So they went down to Bethel.*

*Now the sons of the prophets who were at Bethel came out to Elisha, and said to him, "Do you know that the Lord will take away your master from over you today?"*

*And he said, "Yes, I know; keep silent!"*

*Then Elijah said to him, "Elisha, stay here, please, for the Lord has sent me on to Jericho."*

*But he said, "As the Lord lives, and as your soul lives, I will not leave you!" So they came to Jericho.*

*Now the sons of the prophets who were at Jericho came to Elisha and said to him, "Do you know that the Lord will take away your master from over you today?"*

*So he answered, "Yes, I know; keep silent!"*

*Then Elijah said to him, "Stay here, please, for the Lord has sent me on to the Jordan."*

*But he said, "As the Lord lives, and as your soul lives, I will not leave you!" So the two of them went on. And fifty men of the sons of the prophets went and stood facing them at a distance, while the two of them stood by the Jordan. Now Elijah took his mantle, rolled it up, and struck the water; and it was divided this way and that, so that the two of them crossed over on dry ground.*

*And so it was, when they had crossed over, that Elijah said to Elisha, "Ask! What may I do for you, before I am taken away from you?"*

*Elisha said, "Please let a double portion of your spirit be upon me."*

*So he said, "You have asked a hard thing. Nevertheless, if you see me when I am taken from you, it shall be so for you; but if not, it shall not be so." Then it happened, as they continued on and talked, that suddenly a chariot of fire appeared with horses of fire, and separated the two of them; and Elijah went up by a whirlwind into heaven.*

*And Elisha saw it, and he cried out, "My father, my father, the chariot of Israel and its horsemen!" So he saw him no more. And he took hold of his own clothes and tore them into two pieces. He also took up the mantle of Elijah that had fallen from him, and went back and stood by the bank of the Jordan. Then he took the mantle of Elijah that had fallen from him, and struck the water, and said, "Where is the Lord God of Elijah?" And when he also had struck the water, it was divided this way and that; and Elisha crossed over.*

*Now when the sons of the prophets who were from Jericho saw him, they said, "The spirit of Elijah rests on Elisha." And they came to meet him, and bowed to the ground before him.*

This story culminates the interaction of Elijah with Elisha. It is the ending when Elisha received the mantle that touched him previously. God had told Elijah to anoint Elisha to be a prophet in his place. In other words, Elisha would take the place of Elijah when he had completed his mandate from the Lord. First Kings 19:15-21 gives us the happening of Elijah laying his mantle on Elisha for the first time.

*Then the Lord said to him: "Go, return on your way to the Wilderness of Damascus; and when you arrive, anoint Hazael as king over Syria. Also you shall anoint Jehu the son of Nimshi as king over Israel. And Elisha the son of Shaphat of Abel Meholah you shall anoint as prophet in your place. It shall be that whoever escapes the sword of Hazael, Jehu will kill; and whoever escapes the sword of Jehu, Elisha will kill. Yet I have reserved seven thousand in Israel, all whose knees have not bowed to Baal, and every mouth that has not kissed him."*

*So he departed from there, and found Elisha the son of Shaphat, who was plowing with twelve yoke of oxen before him, and he was with the twelfth. Then Elijah passed by him and threw his mantle on him. And he left the oxen and ran after Elijah, and said, "Please let me kiss my father and my mother, and then I will follow you."*

*And he said to him, "Go back again, for what have I done to you?"*

*So Elisha turned back from him, and took a yoke of oxen and slaughtered them and boiled their flesh, using the oxen's equipment, and gave it to the people, and they ate. Then he arose and followed Elijah, and became his servant.*

Elijah had been in a cave running from Jezebel. This happened because of the conflict on Mount Carmel and the killing of the prophets of Baal. Jezebel threatened revenge and her intent was to kill Elijah. In the midst of Elijah's despair, God commanded him to anoint three people into their function. One of these was Elisha. Elijah found Elisha plowing a field. As Elijah walked by him in the field, he threw his mantle on him. As this mantle touched Elisha, the sense and power of the anointing came on him. It created within him a hunger that would never leave him for the rest of his life. He could no longer be content to plow a field because he had been touched by the power of this mantle.

Elijah's mantle that touched Elisha was simply an outer garment that kept Elijah warm. Yet this mantle carried the anointing of the prophet. The anointing of God is a very real substance that can be imparted. The anointing that was in this mantle was a result of what Elijah carried from God. Just like the anointing was in the garment or mantle of Elijah, it would later be in the bones of Elisha. Years later when Elisha died, his bones were so saturated with the anointing that they raised a dead man to life. We find this in Second Kings 13:20-22.

> *Then Elisha died, and they buried him. And the raiding bands from Moab invaded the land in the spring of the year. So it was, as they were burying a man, that suddenly they spied a band of raiders; and they put the man in the tomb of Elisha; and when the man was let down and touched the bones of Elisha, he revived and stood on his feet.*

This occasion demonstrates that the anointing has the power to saturate garments, mantles, bones, and other substances. This understanding is necessary if we are to recognize why the mantle touching Elisha caused such a response. When this mantle draped and brushed across Elisha as he plowed, the power of the Spirit touched him. It wasn't just a cloth or leather garment touching him. It was the touch of the Holy Spirit that was in this mantle. This one touch of His presence so impacted Elisha that he stopped plowing and ran after Elijah. He asked to be allowed to tell his father and mother goodbye. He intended then to follow after Elijah in pursuit of the mantle.

Elijah's response was quite telling. He said to Elisha, *"Go back. What have I done to you."* There was no fleshly manipulation. There was no luring or promises made. Elijah knew that if Elisha was hungry for the anointing, none of that was necessary. The touch of the anointing would cause Elisha to leave everything in pursuit of the mantle that had touched his life.

Whoever gets the mantle will be those who have an insatiable hunger and thirst for it. Everything else will take a back seat to receiving the mantle. God will allow us to be touched with the mantle of the anointing. This is only to create the hunger for the fullness of it. It will cause no sacrifice to be too great. It will cause illogical decisions to be made. It is all because of that which has touched our lives, which we have decided we simply cannot live without!

This is what happened with Elisha. He went back and slew a yoke of oxen and gave it to the people to eat it. Elisha's occupation had been plowing the field and planting for a harvest. This act was an act of separation. He was making a statement that there was no going back. His life from this point on had one purpose — get the mantle. He would spend the next several years of his life serving Elijah to ultimately receive the mantle in fullness that had touched his life in a moment.

Bible scholars believe that Elisha served Elijah for six years. This service was born out of a hunger for this mantle. We know this is true because when Elijah was taken away, Elisha requested a double portion of what had touched his life. For six years Elisha did mundane things. He clearly left a life of wealth and even privilege. The fact that there were twelve yoke of oxen plowing in his father's field testifies of this prosperity. Elisha was willing to leave it all in pursuit of the mantle. This hunger and pursuit spoke in the Courts of Heaven for him. If we are to get the mantling of the Lord, we must also qualify through a hunger and pursuit. We must qualify through statements of separation that speak for us. All of this is driven by a hunger for that which has touched our lives but we can't live without the fullness of it.

> I ask, Lord, before Your Courts that I might have a hunger for the mantle of the Lord. Even as Elisha hungered and pursued the

mantle, may this same desire be in me. Empower me to acts of separation that testify before You that I desire the mantle more than anything else in life. Allow my longing for this anointing to alter the way I would have otherwise lived my life. Let this speak as a testimony before You that I might receive the mantle of the Lord for my life. In Jesus' Name. Amen.

# CHAPTER 3

# RIGHTLY POSITIONED

As we have seen in the last chapter, Elisha requested a double portion of the anointing and Spirit that was on Elijah. This hunger and thirst spoke on his behalf in the Courts of Heaven. God loves it when we believe big. However, there must be a corresponding obedience to obtain this level of mantling. Elisha had this operating in his life. He had served Elijah for six years out of his hunger for the mantle. As the time drew near for the impartation of this mantle, there was final test that he had to pass.

When we pass the testing of the Lord, we qualify before His Courts for mantles. As we have read in the last chapter, Elijah told Elisha to stay and not bother to go on this journey with him. However, Elisha would not leave the side of Elijah. Elisha understood how important it was to be rightly positioned to receive the mantle. If he was out of position, all that he served for, believed for, and waited on would be lost. However, if he could be righty positioned he would get the desire of his heart. When Elijah told him to just stay and not put himself out in Second Kings 2:1-2, Elisha made a significant statement.

> *And it came to pass, when the Lord was about to take up Elijah into heaven by a whirlwind, that Elijah went with Elisha from Gilgal. Then Elijah said to Elisha, "Stay here, please, for the Lord has sent me on to Bethel."*
>
> *But Elisha said, "As the Lord lives, and as your soul lives, I will not leave you!" So they went down to Bethel.*

Notice that Elisha declared *as the Lord lives and as your soul lives*. Elisha's commitment was to God and the one who represented God in his life. This is very important. If we don't have these same commitments, we can miss the mantle God has for us. Many people have no problem being committed to God. Their problem is being committed to the one God has set in their life. It's easy, at times, to serve a perfect God, but not so easy to serve an imperfect vessel representing God to us. However, Elisha knew that the mantle he was to receive was coming from God *through* the one God had given him to serve. This is vitally important. Otherwise, we can miss the moment in time when the mantle is to be imparted.

When it appeared that Elijah was being kind and giving Elisha some time off, Elisha recognized the test. Was he going to stay true and committed on both levels? Or was he going to bail out at the last moment and miss what he had invested for the last six years? There really was no decision to be made. It had already been made six years before. If Elijah was alive and breathing on the planet, Elisha would be with him.

The second thing that was crucial in this moment was—would Elisha be able to discern the prophetic time he was in? What was it that made this time different from the last six years? It was simply that Elijah was leaving and it was the moment of potential impartation. Elisha had to be able to discern and know this. We are told that it was the time when Elijah would leave in a whirlwind. Could Elisha discern this in the spirit without being told in the natural? Elijah knew it was time. But did Elisha? Elijah didn't tell him. If he was to qualify for the mantle, he must be able to discern the times and seasons.

These times are called *kairos times* in the Bible. *Kairos* is a Greek word that means "a moment of time." Whereas the Greek word *chronos* means "a span of time." The last six years had been *chronos* or a *span of time* for Elisha. We all live our life in *chronos*. This is the time we take care of business and stay faithful and diligent. However, there are then those moments of time—*kairos*. What happens in these prophetic times determines what our future will be. The sad fact is many people don't discern when *chronos* becomes *kairos*. This is what Jesus spoke of in Luke 19:41-44. He was weeping because they had missed their *kairos* moment.

> *Now as He drew near, He saw the city and wept over it, saying, "If you had known, even you, especially in this your day, the things that make for your peace! But now they are hidden from your eyes. For days will come upon you when your enemies will build an embankment around you, surround you and close you in on every side, and level you, and your children within you, to the ground; and they will not leave in you one stone upon another, because you did not know the time of your visitation."*

This "time of your visitation" is *kairos*. Jesus was telling them that because they missed their moment, devastation was coming. Recognizing *kairos* is essential. This was what Elisha had to do. Getting your mantle requires recognizing the prophetic moment you are in and not being distracted. Getting distracted in a *kairos* moment is more than unfortunate. It is life-changing for the negative. However, if we can recognize it and move in agreement with it, what we have lived for can become ours. This is what Elisha was able to do. He had become spiritually sensitive and knew the times he was in and what he was to be doing. This resulted in the double portion mantle secured.

The sons of the prophets would come to him in each place he and Elijah journeyed. They would ask if he knew Elijah was leaving. He would say to them that he did know and that they should be quiet. One of the places we see this is Second Kings 2:5.

> *Now the sons of the prophets who were at Jericho came to Elisha and said to him, "Do you know that the Lord will take away your master from over you today?"*
>
> *So he answered, "Yes, I know; keep silent!"*

When something is stirring in the spirit world, anyone who is prophetic can pick it up. The sons of the prophets were those trained to operate in the prophetic. It was a school that Elijah most likely oversaw. They were discerning in the spirit world that Elijah was about to be taken away. Notice that Elisha was not dependent on what others were discerning prophetically. He was himself able to know what was happening in the unseen realm.

If we are to get the mantles of the Lord, this is imperative. We must develop our own prophetic sensitivity.

This is not to say that we don't interact with other prophetic people. However, Elisha knew what was happening because he had paid the price to develop his own prophetic abilities. This allowed him to know what was occurring in this moment. We must pay the price of intimacy and surrender to know what is happening in given moments. When we do, we are no longer at the mercy of what others are telling us prophetically. We can hear the Lord ourselves. This is important when it comes to receiving the double portion mantle of the Lord. Elisha was not positioning himself because of the prophetic word of others. He was positioning himself because of what he himself was hearing. So must we as well. We must learn to listen and trust what we are hearing. It will allow us to be rightly set and positioned for the securing of the mantle of the Lord.

> As I come before Your Courts, Lord, I ask that my commitment to You and my commitment to those You have joined me to might speak before You. May I always be faithful to You but also serve those who represent You in my life. Allow me, Lord, to be rightly positioned through this obedience. Let me receive the mantling of the Lord.
>
> I also ask that I might be rightly set through prophetically discerning the kairos times

of God. Help me, Lord, to walk in intimacy and surrender to You that I might discern the times and season of the Lord. Let me not miss my kairos moment of impartation of the mantling of the Lord.

Would You allow my right positioning as a result of my obedience to speak in Your Courts? Would You allow this to testify of me that I might be honored with the mantle of the Lord on my life. In Jesus' Name, amen.

# CHAPTER 4

# ASKING THE HARD THING

A s Elijah and Elisha continued their journey together, Elijah finally acknowledged that he was leaving. Up until this time, it had been required of Elisha to discern this by the Spirit. In Second Kings 2:8-10 we see Elijah addressing Elisha.

> *Now Elijah took his mantle, rolled it up, and struck the water; and it was divided this way and that, so that the two of them crossed over on dry ground.*
>
> *And so it was, when they had crossed over, that Elijah said to Elisha, "Ask! What may I do for you, before I am taken away from you?"*
>
> *Elisha said, "Please let a double portion of your spirit be upon me."*
>
> *So he said, "You have asked a hard thing. Nevertheless, if you see me when I am taken from you, it shall be so for you; but if not, it shall not be so."*

As it became time for the impartation, Elijah allowed Elisha to ask anything that he wanted. There are only a few times in scripture when we see this kind of opportunity being given. Solomon was allowed to ask for whatever he desired in First Kings 3:4-9.

> *Now the king went to Gibeon to sacrifice there, for that was the great high place: Solomon offered a thousand burnt offerings on that altar. At Gibeon the Lord appeared to Solomon in a dream by night; and God said, "Ask! What shall I give you?"*
>
> *And Solomon said: "You have shown great mercy to Your servant David my father, because he walked before You in truth, in righteousness, and in uprightness of heart with You; You have continued this great kindness for him, and You have given him a son to sit on his throne, as it is this day. Now, O Lord my God, You have made Your servant king instead of my father David, but I am a little child; I do not know how to go out or come in. And Your servant is in the midst of Your people whom You have chosen, a great people, too numerous to be numbered or counted. Therefore give to Your servant an understanding heart to judge Your people, that I may discern between good and evil. For who is able to judge this great people of Yours?"*

As a result of Solomon's extravagant offering, God came to him in a dream. His offering speaking before the Lord caused God to remember him. We must never underestimate the power of an extravagant offering. Finances and sacrifices speak in the Courts of Heaven for us. An offering that is from a true and good heart testifies in the Courts of Heaven for us. Matthew 5:23-25 gives us a glimpse of this.

> *Therefore if you bring your gift to the altar, and there remember that your brother has something against you, leave your gift there before the altar, and go your way. First be reconciled to your brother, and then come and offer your gift. Agree with your adversary quickly, while you are on the way with him, lest your adversary deliver you to the judge, the judge hand you over to the officer, and you be thrown into prison.*

Jesus connects offerings with judicial activity. We are told that we must not bring an offering if there is a conflict with another person. We are to leave our offering and seek reconciliation first. We are told if our offering is given with a wrong heart toward another, it can result in a judgment against us. We can be thrown into a spiritual prison because of a wrong spirit and attitude as we gave. This is because offerings have testimonies attached to them. The state and condition of our heart as we bring our offering determines the testimony connected to it. This is why when Solomon brought such an acceptable offering, it caused God to grant him complete freedom to ask whatever he desired.

Our offerings have this power before the Lord. My money has a voice in the Courts of Heaven. We see this as well in James 5:1-4. James exhorts that money that is held back is crying. It is speaking in the spiritual dimensions of the Courts of Heaven.

> *Come now, you rich, weep and howl for your miseries that are coming upon you! Your riches are corrupted, and your garments are moth-eaten. Your gold and silver are corroded, and their corrosion will be a witness against you and will eat your flesh like fire. You have heaped up treasure in the last days. Indeed the wages of the laborers who mowed your fields, which you kept back by fraud, cry out; and the cries of the reapers have reached the ears of the Lord of Sabaoth.*

When money is held back from its rightful steward, it will speak against the oppression. Notice that the *wages* that were kept back through fraud are *crying out.* The testimony of the *wages,* mixed with the cries of the reapers, come before the Lord. This scripture says this will allow judgment against oppressive economic systems. In other words, that which is *rigged* and will not allow people to prosper is judged by God. If we would learn to agree with the voice of money, we could see judgment touch what is stopping our prosperity.

I am speaking of this with regard to the sound/voice/testimony that money has. When Solomon brought his offering of righteousness, it spoke for him in the Courts of Heaven. The result was God coming to him at night and giving him *carte blanche*. He was allowed to ask for anything and have it become reality. Our God is able to do the *hard thing*. This is what Elijah is offering Elisha. He is allowed to ask whatever he wants before Elijah leaves. In these moments, our hearts need to be prepared. These moments can determine the rest of our lives. By the way, Solomon's request so pleased God that He even gave him what he didn't ask. We see this in First Kings 3:10-13.

> *The speech pleased the Lord, that Solomon had asked this thing. Then God said to him: "Because you have asked this thing, and have not asked long life for yourself, nor have asked riches for yourself, nor have asked the life of your enemies, but have asked for yourself understanding to discern justice, behold, I have done according to your words; see, I have given you a wise and understanding heart, so that there has not been*

*anyone like you before you, nor shall any like you arise after you. And I have also given you what you have not asked: both riches and honor, so that there shall not be anyone like you among the kings all your days.*

His request came out of a prepared heart. His heart was so right toward the Lord and the people of God that he asked the right thing. The result was God gave him much more than he asked of Him.

When Elisha was told by Elijah to *ask* whatever he wanted, this was a moment of testing. What would he ask? He had seen the miracles and the power of the Lord flow through Elijah. I would have to say that if I had seen and witnessed this, I'm not sure it would have even occurred to me to ask for double. Yet this is what Elisha did. He asked for a double portion of the spirit that was on Elijah. There was clearly a faith level in Elisha that could believe for this. Yet Elijah seemed hesitant to promise this to Elisha. He placed a stipulation on Elisha receiving the double portion. He had to *see* him when he left. If he saw him, he would get what he had requested.We know that Elisha did in fact witness the translation of Elijah. He saw him ascend in the chariots of heaven into eternity. The mantle did fall back to him that would carry the double portion of the anointing and spirit of Elijah. This whole principle of *seeing* is very important. We can only receive from what we can *see*. This is what God promised Abraham. He was told in Genesis 13:14-15 that he would have as far as he could see.

> *And the Lord said to Abram, after Lot had sepa-*
> *rated from him: "Lift your eyes now and look from*
> *the place where you are — northward, southward,*
> *eastward, and westward; for all the land which you*
> *see I give to you and your descendants forever."*

Abraham was told that the land he could *see* would be his and his descendants'. The limits were determined by what he could *see*. We must develop spiritual perception. We must perceive things in our spirit and *see*. This causes faith to arise in our hearts. From this seeing, we contend for and secure the promises of God. Our ability to *see* comes from the Holy Spirit. We are told in First Corinthians 2:9-12 that this spiritual perception is required.

> *But as it is written:*
> *"Eye has not seen, nor ear heard,*
> *Nor have entered into the heart of man*
> *The things which God has prepared for those who*
> *love Him."*

*But God has revealed them to us through His Spirit. For the Spirit searches all things, yes, the deep things of God. For what man knows the things of a man except the spirit of the man which is in him? Even so no one knows the things of God except the Spirit of God. Now we have received, not the spirit of the world, but the Spirit who is from God, that we might know the things that have been freely given to us by God.*

Notice that it is not natural perception required. Our natural eye hasn't seen, nor have our natural ears heard. Even in the natural our hearts haven't understood. This lets us know that *perceiving* is a spiritual happening. The Holy Spirit that is in God and in us unveils the deep things of God. We must *know* the things freely given to us before we can obtain them. We must *see* them in the spirit through the revelation of the Holy Spirit. As this happens, we can have what we see! This is what happened with Elisha. He saw! As a result he received the mantle and the double portion of the anointing that had rested on Elijah. We should ask for any dullness of spirit to be removed from us so that we might perceive that which is freely given us. Jesus' work on the cross and through His resurrection has legally released all things to us. However, we can only get them through the application of the Holy Spirit. As we *see* what belongs to us legally because of what Jesus has done, we can then ask with great faith. We can be like Elisha and ask the hard thing that many others might miss. The Lord is looking for those who can receive and carry these mantles from the Lord.

Lord, as I come into Your Courts I desire a faith to ask for the hard thing. Would You allow my heart to be stirred with great faith to believe You? I repent for any and all dullness of heart that would prohibit me from perceiving what is legally mine. Lord, thank You that there are awesome things that belong to me legally because of what You have done. I ask that I might perceive and see them, that I could receive them from You. Even as Elisha saw and received, would You allow this for me as well?

Would You prepare my heart to ask out of what I see? Let there be in me, as there was in Solomon, a heart to ask that which pleases You. May I have the kind of heart that allows my petition and request before You to bless Your heart. Let my heart have the testimony before Your Courts that grants me status in this place. May my life be that which You can entrust with the mantling of the Lord for Your divine purposes. In Jesus' Name, amen.

# CHAPTER 5

# WHERE IS THE GOD OF ELIJAH?

A s the mantle fell back from the whisking away of Elijah, Elisha had to pick it up. There is always a need to pick up what has been given. Many people either don't perceive what has been released or they don't have the faith and courage to pick it up. Elisha did several things in the process of picking up the mantle and learning to use it. Again Second Kings 2:12-14 shows this process that Elisha walked through.

> And Elisha saw it, and he cried out, "My father, my father, the chariot of Israel and its horsemen!" So he saw him no more. And he took hold of his own clothes and tore them into two pieces. He also took up the mantle of Elijah that had fallen from him, and went back and stood by the bank of the Jordan. Then he took the mantle of Elijah that had fallen from him, and struck the water, and

*said, "Where is the Lord God of Elijah?" And*
*when he also had struck the water, it was divided*
*this way and that; and Elisha crossed over.*

The first thing Elisha did as Elijah was taken away
was he tore his garments. The tearing of the garments
is a sign of brokenness, repentance, and surrender. We
are told in Joel 2:13 to tear our hearts in repentance and
not our garments.

*So rend your heart, and not your garments;*

*Return to the Lord your God,*

*For He is gracious and merciful,*

*Slow to anger, and of great kindness;*

*And He relents from doing harm.*

The tearing of garments was a symbolic gesture
of the brokenness in the heart. When I speak of brokenness, I am not talking about tragedy occurring.
Brokenness is simply a spiritual state where His will
has been enthroned over our will. When Elisha tore his
garment, it was a display of what was happening in his
heart. Not only was he surrendering completely and
ultimately to God, he was also mourning the loss of
Elijah. The rending of garments also speaks of a deep
sorrow and grief. After six years of service, communion, and commitment, Elijah was not just someone he

wanted something from. As he left, Elisha cried out, *"My father, my father."* Elijah had become a father to Elisha. There was a deep pain in Elisha's heart as Elijah left. This produced a brokenness and surrender. I can think of another place in scripture where the loss of someone greatly loved had a similar effect. We are told in Isaiah 6:1 that the prophet had an intense encounter in the year of a beloved king's death.

> *In the year that King Uzziah died, I saw the Lord sitting on a throne, high and lifted up, and the train of His robe filled the temple.*

There seems to be a connection between the loss of someone, the grief associated with it, and the new spiritual realm accessed. Isaiah loved King Uzziah. There was something about the struggle brought on by his passing that opened Isaiah to this realm of glory. This seems to be what was happening with Elisha. There was a mourning at the transitioning of Elijah. The pain of his passing was touching Elisha in a great way. He realized that he would not see him again in this life. In the midst of the mantle received, there was a struggle with the loss he was feeling. Let me encourage anyone who is going through a grief process. Allow the grief cycle to open for you an encounter in the heavenly realm. God always turns all things to good if we allow Him. He is able to redeem this place of grief and open visitations that deposit a great wealth of spiritual power.

Elisha then picked up the mantle of the Lord. Picking up the mantle being offered is an activity of faith. The Lord can release the mantle, but we must grab hold of it through aggressive faith. One of the things I have noticed through the years is a passivity in the people of God. I have often said, *"Faith is not a quiet believing, but a violent pursuit."* In other words, we are going to get what we know is ours, regardless of what might stand in the way.

When I speak of a *violent pursuit,* I am obviously not talking of violence or aggression in the physical realm. I am talking of a passion that is unquenchable. Many years ago, when I was seeking to pioneer a work that God had commissioned me with, I was in a time of prayer. There happened to be a man in that prayer time that day who didn't much care for me. He felt I wasn't giving his son, who worked for me, a fair shake. So this man wasn't a big fan. However, he told me later that as he looked at me as I stood with my face to the wall crying out to God, the Lord spoke to him about me. He said that as I stood praying, the Lord said to him about me, *"See this man? He will not be denied."*

I was amazed at what he was saying because of the attitude he had toward me. Yet the Lord was letting me know that my pursuit and diligence would be rewarded. My faith and patience to endure and not give up would obtain the promises of God. If we are to pick up the mantles of the Lord, it will require this kind of faith and believing. If we don't stop or quit, we will obtain!

Another important idea concerning the picking up of mantles is *worship.* There is an occasion in scripture when a woman's son died. This son had been prophetically promised by Elisha. The son had been born, but then after a few years he died. This woman then went to the prophet and brought him back to the body of her dead son. The prophet went into the room where the dead boy now lay. In Second Kings 4:32-37, we see this story unfold.

> *When Elisha came into the house, there was the child, lying dead on his bed. He went in therefore, shut the door behind the two of them, and prayed to the Lord. And he went up and lay on the child, and put his mouth on his mouth, his eyes on his eyes, and his hands on his hands; and he stretched himself out on the child, and the flesh of the child became warm. He returned and walked back and forth in the house, and again went up and stretched himself out on him; then the child sneezed seven times, and the child opened his*

*eyes. And he called Gehazi and said, "Call this Shunammite woman." So he called her. And when she came in to him, he said, "Pick up your son." So she went in, fell at his feet, and bowed to the ground; then she picked up her son and went out.*

Notice when the woman came in after her son's resurrection that in the act of *picking* him up, she bowed in worship. Worship is one of the main ways we *pick up* things in the spirit realm. As we worship deeply in the Lord, we grab hold of the resurrection power of the Lord. This really is what mantles are. They carry the resurrection power of Jesus in given areas. I would encourage all of us to learn to worship and adore the Lord in ever-deepening ways. As we do, we will pick up mantles and anointing that will empower us in our assignments from the Lord.

As we get lost in the worship of Jesus, quite often there is an unknown thing occurring. There is an impartation of the resurrection life of God that is being deposited in our spirits. From this deposit, we will be able to live, function, and operate on a higher level. We are picking up the mantles of the Lord from a deep place of communion with the Lord.

John G. Lake recorded his receiving of the anointing/ mantle of the Lord. Even before he was baptized in the

Holy Spirit, he functioned in healing by faith. He had a revelation of what Jesus had done for us on the cross. He saw many dynamic healings simply by operating in faith in who Jesus is and what He has done. However, Lake was seeking for the baptism of the Holy Spirit. He had not yet received this mantle of empowerment when he and his preaching partner went to pray for the healing of a person. Lake's account of this experience is that his preaching partner was sharing how to receive healing with the one who needed to be healed. Lake records that as this was occurring he was sitting in a chair listening. Suddenly, the Holy Spirit fell on Lake, and he began to tremble so excessively that he thought he might shake himself from the chair. As this weight of the Spirit of the Lord came, he began to speak in other tongues. He was gloriously baptized in the Spirit of the Lord.His retrospective look at what happened in those moments is revealing. He said that in those moments, he received a deposit of the Lord into his spirit. Even though the intensity of that moment was not repeated, what he received then empowered him for the rest of his life. We do not always have to have these dynamic experiences to carry a mantle. The glory in a moment can so touch us that a mantle has been imparted and picked up for the rest of our days. This is what happened with John G. Lake. From this mantle, the power of the Lord touched South Africa; Spokane,

Washington; and many other places through Lake and the ministry he birthed. There are those who reported that Lake functioned in a power of the Spirit reminiscent of biblical days. May we receive and pick up the mantles of God in this way.

Once Elisha picked up the mantle, he needed to learn to use it. Hence his statement, *"Where is the Lord God of Elijah?"* As Elisha approached the Jordan River with the newly acquired mantle, he now had to use it. He took the mantle, rolled it up, and hit the river with it. As he spoke the word, the river divided this way and that, and he walked across on dry ground. Using the mantles we have received is a learned process. It is interesting that when rivers to swim in were seen in Ezekiel 47:2-5, there was a man who not only measured out a new level but brought the prophet through it as well.

> *He brought me out by way of the north gate, and led me around on the outside to the outer gateway that faces east; and there was water, running out on the right side.*
>
> *And when the man went out to the east with the line in his hand, he measured one thousand cubits, and he brought me through the waters; the water came up to my ankles. Again he measured one thousand and brought me through the*

*waters; the water came up to my knees. Again he*
*measured one thousand and brought me through;*
*the water came up to my waist. Again he mea-*
*sured one thousand, and it was a river that I*
*could not cross; for the water was too deep, water*
*in which one must swim, a river that could not*
*be crossed.*

The new levels of water speak of greater dimensions of the Holy Spirit to flow and move in. As each dimension was measured out, the one doing this also *brought me through the waters*. This speaks of not only new levels being granted but also a learning to flow in them. The same Spirit who measures out the new levels also teaches us to move in these levels. Any mantle we receive from the Lord will require us learning to function in it effectively.

We can see the same idea in Hannah making a new coat for Samuel each year. Samuel had been dedicated to the Lord even before his conception. In obedience and fulfillment of her vow, Hannah gave him to the Lord. He lived in the same place as Eli the High Priest. Every year when Hannah and the family came to worship, she brought him a new robe for the year. We find this in First Samuel 2:19.

*Moreover his mother used to make him a little*
*robe, and bring it to him year by year when she*

*came up with her husband to offer the yearly sacrifice.*

The word *robe* is the Hebrew word *m'iyl*. It means "a covering, an upper and outer garment, a mantle." Every year she brought him a *new mantle*. For the mantle to suffice for the entire year for a growing boy, it had to be made big enough for the boy to *grow into*. This means the *mantle* was too big when first placed on him. He had to *grow into* it. This is true for us as well. Any mantle we receive from the Lord must be grown into. This means we develop faith to operate in the level of mantling we have received. We learn to move in the faith level and the means unveiled by the Holy Spirit. As we do, we will grow into the full level of operation in the mantling of the Lord.

Though he had witnessed Elijah using the anointing/mantle of the Lord for six years, Elisha now had to learn himself. He would go on to use this mantle in tremendous ways. Elisha was recorded to have done twice as many miracles as Elijah did. He did, in fact, receive the double portion of the mantling of God. He also learned to operate in it under the direction of the Spirit of the Lord. As we receive the mantles of God, may we be dedicated in using them to the fullness of what we have received. The effect of the mantle we receive and walk in will be seen in our realms of faith and grace. We will see how to get the full effect of a mantle operating in our life in the next chapter.

As I approach Your Courts, Lord, I ask that anything that is necessary to receive the mantling of God would be done in my life. I ask that I might be a person of pursuit who desires the mantle of the Lord. May it be recorded before You that there is no sacrifice too great. Even as Elisha, I would forsake all to receive the mantle of Your glory and presence.

Let is also be known and recorded before Your Courts that I honor those who have carried the mantles before me. Even as Elisha honored Elijah, I value those who paid the price for these mantles.

I also allow any grief from loss of loved ones, reputation, things, or other precious and valued items or issues to be used to prepare me for this mantle. Even as Elisha mourned the loss of Elijah and tore his garment, may brokenness be in me. May I be prepared in the inner man to carry the mantle of my God.

I also by faith pick up the mantle of God for me. May it be known that I worship You in deep adoration. As I worship You, may the mantle of God be deposited in my spirit. May I be empowered as never before.

I also purpose to act with the mantle in faith. I thank You that You allow me to grow into a full place of the use of this mantle. May there be a great demonstration of the glory and power of God as this mantle is imparted, activated, and used. In Jesus' Name, amen.

# CHAPTER 6

# GRACE: MANTLES' HIDDEN GIFT

As with anything we receive from the Lord, the effectiveness of it will be determined by our faith and consecration. So it is with the mantles of God deposited in our life. We must use them to the greatest potential. Paul actually spoke of this in his own life. In First Corinthians 15:10, Paul declared the grace he received was used to work greatly.

> *But by the grace of God I am what I am, and His grace toward me was not in vain; but I labored more abundantly than they all, yet not I, but the grace of God which was with me.*

Paul was aware that the grace of God had produced in him who he was. He then declared that from what he had received he labored more abundantly than everyone else. In other words, he chose to pull from the mantle and accomplish the assignment granted him from the Lord. Notice that Paul spoke of *grace* that created this in him. With every mantle received, there is grace that accompanies it. Mantles from the Lord will have measures of grace they deposit in our lives. Grace is not just something we are saved by. Grace is the empowerment of God in our lives. As mantles settle on us, there will be a fresh realm of grace that touches our lives. We will use the mantles of His presence and glory from the grace of God they have placed in our lives. It would behoove us to have an understanding of grace as it is associated with mantles.

One of the reasons we are aware of the association of mantles and grace is because grace determines the gifting we carry. First Peter 4:10 lets us know that the grace of God has many different facets.

> *As each one has received a gift, minister it to one another, as good stewards of the manifold grace of God.*

The word *manifold* is the Greek word *poikilos*. It means "motley, various in character, different." In other words, the grace of God has many different ideas, dimensions, and realms. We know that according to John 1:17 Jesus is the source of grace.

> *For the law was given through Moses, but grace and truth came through Jesus Christ.*

Just like Jesus is the *truth* (see John 14:6), Jesus is also *grace* personified. As Jesus is revealed and known in His fullness, there are abundant levels of grace received and imparted. First Peter 1:13 tells us that the deeper our revelation of Jesus goes, the more grace we obtain.

> *Therefore gird up the loins of your mind, be sober, and rest your hope fully upon the grace that is to be brought to you at the revelation of Jesus Christ.*

Clearly this is speaking of the second coming of Jesus. When He appears there will be a fullness of grace that becomes ours. However, the principle is true today. The greater our revelation of Jesus is, the more grace we apprehend. This empowers our life on ever-increasing levels. This is why mantles and grace are so connected. When a mantle from the Lord is entrusted to us, there will be a grace appointed that we might operate in it effectively. Without a grace from God, the mantle we have received could be misused and the intent of the Lord frustrated. When we have the grace that is joined to the mantle, we have every-thing we need to be faithful.

As a result of Jesus being the source of all grace or even grace Himself, just as there are various mantles, the grace attached to individual mantles is different. Anytime I read the word *manifold*, I always think of the manifold on a car engine. If the car has eight cylinders or pistons, each piston will feed into the *manifold*. This allows the exhaust produced by the car's operation to flow from the manifold into the exhaust system and out the tailpipe. What originates in eight different cylinders of the engine culminates and dovetails into one place. This is a reverse idea of the grace of God. The grace of God originates in Jesus. However, it will be dispensed out in various ways, means, and natures. This allows different aspects of grace to be distributed to us as the body of Christ. Each grace has a piece of His nature and power. Though they are difference, they come from the same source. We see this in Romans 12:6-8. In these verses we see the grace that comes from Jesus being dispensed in seven different ways.

> *Having then gifts differing according to the grace that is given to us, let us use them: if prophecy, let us prophesy in proportion to our faith; or ministry, let us use it in our ministering; he who teaches, in teaching; he who exhorts, in exhortation; he who gives, with liberality; he who leads, with diligence; he who shows mercy, with cheerfulness.*

Notice that grace results in different giftings received and operated in. Could it be that each one of these giftings mentioned are the result of mantles with accompanying grace? We are told that as a result of a specific grace received, some might operate *prophetically.* Another might be given to *service/ministry.* Still someone else might have a propensity toward *teaching.* Another will operate in *exhortation* from grace received. Then there are those who are *givers* who greatly finance the work of God. There is also a grace for *administration/organization/leadership.* Finally, we are told about those who show *mercy* as a result of the grace on their life.

This is an understanding of the *manifold* grace of God and the different functions it empowers. Could it be that this grace is because of a mantle that is obtained? The result works into our life an inclination and strength to minister and be effective in these realms. A friend of mine pointed out that when a mantle it received it not only empowers us but changes us into the image of the mantle. I believe this. This is what happened to Saul, the first king of Israel. When Samuel anointed him to be king, he prophetically told him what would happen in a very short time. First Samuel 10:5-7 tells us of these instructions and information the prophet gave to Saul.

> *After that you shall come to the hill of God where the Philistine garrison is. And it will happen, when you have come there to the city, that you*

*will meet a group of prophets coming down from the high place with a stringed instrument, a tambourine, a flute, and a harp before them; and they will be prophesying. Then the Spirit of the Lord will come upon you, and you will prophesy with them and be turned into another man. And let it be, when these signs come to you, that you do as the occasion demands; for God is with you.*

Saul was told that the spirit of God would fall on him as he encountered this group of prophets. If you will, as the mantle touched his life, he was changed into another man. The prophetic mantle he received began to fashion who he was as it touched him. This is because a mantle doesn't just empower us for our assignment, it changes us into the likeness and image required for the assignment. This is probably because of the grace bestowed on our lives that is connected with the mantle. Remember that Paul said, "*I am who I am by the grace of God.*" He was declaring that the grace that had touched his life had fashioned and formed him for the purposes of God.

It seemed Paul was able to operate in the grace afforded him as a result of the mantles he had received. He was able to fulfill his purpose and get a full reward. He declared in Second Timothy 4:5-8 that he had a crown awaiting him because of his faithfulness with the mantle and the assignment it empowered him to complete.

> *But you be watchful in all things, endure afflic-*
> *tions, do the work of an evangelist, fulfill your*
> *ministry. For I am already being poured out as a*
> *drink offering, and the time of my departure is at*
> *hand. I have fought the good fight, I have finished*
> *the race, I have kept the faith. Finally, there is*
> *laid up for me the crown of righteousness, which*
> *the Lord, the righteous Judge, will give to me on*
> *that Day, and not to me only but also to all who*
> *have loved His appearing.*

Paul was challenging Timothy, his son in the faith, to not fall short. He was exhorting him to fulfill his ministry — in other words, to use fully the grace he has received to operate in the mantle, to completely satisfy the desire of God. Then he used himself as an example. He declared that he had been totally faithful to the call and desire of God over his life. He had used the mantle and the grace associated with it to complete His work. As a result of this, he had a crown of righteousness waiting for him.

Even as I write this, this is my longing as well: when I stand before Him, that I will be judged as faithful to Him and the work. I will not have pulled up short or stopped prematurely. I will have operated in the mantles of God and discovered the grace joined to them. This will have empowered me in my yearning to be true to the Lord and fulfill the ministry granted me. May it be true for us all.

> As I come before the Courts of Heaven, I am requesting the mantling of the Lord to fulfill every assignment given to me before God. Would You allow it to be recorded that I desire to complete the work given me? I request that a fresh mantling of the Lord would come on me. I ask that the grace attached to this mantle would empower me and strengthen me to steward rightly the mantle of God. May I walk faithfully before You that I might receive a crown of righteousness even as spoken of in Your Word. I do not want to fall short and not complete my assignment. Let Your mantle and Your grace come on my life this day, in Jesus' Name, amen.

# CHAPTER 7

# MANTLES AND THE ANOINTING OIL

When we speak of mantles, we are speaking of the anointing of God over our life. In other words, when we are mantled by the Lord, there will be an anointing that will empower us for service. This is why Elisha received the mantle of Elijah. It was saturated with the anointing that the prophet had walked in. In receiving the mantle, he received the anointing of God over his life. We see the anointing being spoken of in Exodus 30:22-33. Moses is commanded to have this anointing oil made.

> *Moreover the Lord spoke to Moses, saying: "Also take for yourself quality spices — five hundred shekels of liquid myrrh, half as much sweet-smelling cinnamon (two hundred and fifty shekels), two hundred and fifty shekels of sweet-smelling cane, five hundred shekels of cassia, according to*

*the shekel of the sanctuary, and a hin of olive oil. And you shall make from these a holy anointing oil, an ointment compounded according to the art of the perfumer. It shall be a holy anointing oil. With it you shall anoint the tabernacle of meeting and the ark of the Testimony; the table and all its utensils, the lampstand and its utensils, and the altar of incense; the altar of burnt offering with all its utensils, and the laver and its base. You shall consecrate them, that they may be most holy; whatever touches them must be holy. And you shall anoint Aaron and his sons, and consecrate them, that they may minister to Me as priests.*

*"And you shall speak to the children of Israel, saying: 'This shall be a holy anointing oil to Me throughout your generations. It shall not be poured on man's flesh; nor shall you make any other like it, according to its composition. It is holy, and it shall be holy to you. Whoever compounds any like it, or whoever puts any of it on an outsider, shall be cut off from his people.'"*

There is great understanding concerning the anointing in these scriptures. There is also something we can see that we need to present in the Courts of Heaven. The mishandling and wrong stewardship of past anointing has allowed the devil a case against us. We can go before the Courts of Heaven and see this case dismissed. This will allow us not to be deemed disqualified for the fresh mantling of the Lord.

The anointing oil was prepared to anoint many things and make them holy. We see this declared several times. Everything from the utensils to the tabernacle itself was to be anointed with this oil. As these were anointed, they were deemed set apart and consecrated for service to the Lord. They were dedicated to the Lord and His purposes. When something is called *holy* it doesn't just mean undefiled. It means it is given to the Lord alone for His divine intent. The anointing oil says this now belongs to the Lord. This is why, when we are saved, we should receive the Holy Spirit. It is He who is coming to take possession of what has been redeemed by the blood. Ephesians 1:13 lets us know that when we believed, the Holy Spirit sealed us.

> *In Him you also trusted, after you heard the word of truth, the gospel of your salvation; in whom also, having believed, you were sealed with the Holy Spirit of promise.*

The Holy Spirit confirms and lets us know that we are the Lord's. The word seal is the Greek word sphragizo. It means "a stamp with a private mark, security, or preservation." The anointing of the Holy Spirit secures us for all eternity. He fights and opposes anything that would endeavor to take what now belongs to God from Him. This is why we feel conviction. It is the Holy Spirit and His anointing that is contending with our flesh, the devil, the world, and any other thing trying to claim what is the Lord's. Once anointed with the power of His presence, we are stamped with His private mark. The Holy Spirit will contend with anything that would seek to steal what is the Lord's.

In these verses in Exodus we see the "ingredients" to the anointing oil. They speak to us of different aspects of being anointed of God. Of course, we are speaking of what happens when we are mantled by God with His precious Spirit. There were five different spices and oils that were to be used to prepare the anointing oil. They used myrrh, sweet cinnamon, sweet smelling cane, cassia, and olive oil. These spices and oil were mixed together underneath the oversight of the perfumer. Exodus 30:25 makes this clear.

> *And you shall make from these a holy anointing oil, an ointment compounded according to the art of the perfumer. It shall be a holy anointing oil.*

The Holy Spirit is the master *perfumer*. He is the one who *mixes* together these ingredients into the precious anointing of God. As He is the *perfumer*, the anointing doesn't only empower, it puts an aroma on our life as well. Paul spoke to this when he said that they were an aroma of life to some and death to others. Second Corinthians 2:15-16 declares this.

> *For we are to God the fragrance of Christ among those who are being saved and among those who are perishing. To the one we are the aroma of death leading to death, and to the other the aroma of life leading to life. And who is sufficient for these things?*

We are to be the *fragrance of Christ* to all. Our lives are to release the essence of His perfume. The sweet smell of who He is should be carried from our lives. Fragrances and smells are very powerful. I believe the fragrance of Christ is the result of the anointing of God. When we are anointed, our lives will have the sweet aroma of Him. What I mean by this is that our disposition, personality, and presence should be filled with a sense of His presence. For instance, when Esther went before the king, she had been heavily *bathed* in anointing. Esther 2:12 gives us some insight to the preparation of Esther to be presented to the king. Remember that she was auditioning to be the queen in the place of the one who had rebelled. She had spent 12 months in purification and beautification.

*Each young woman's turn came to go in to
King Ahasuerus after she had completed twelve
months' preparation, according to the regula-
tions for the women, for thus were the days of
their preparation apportioned: six months with
oil of myrrh, and six months with perfumes and
preparations for beautifying women.*

It is not too much of a stretch to believe that Esther
was so *anointed* from her 12 months of beautification
that the aroma of who she was went ahead of her. In
other words, her fragrance entered the room before
she did. The aroma surrounding her introduced her to
the king. She was, in fact, chosen by the king to be his
queen. The aroma of the anointing of God on our lives
can introduce us as well. It can prepare the way for us.
Another place where we see the aroma of the anointing is when Mary broke the alabaster box in John 12:3.
Jesus had raised Lazarus from the dead. They were
now in the house of Martha and Mary. As they sat at
the table in communion, Mary suddenly came with a
pound of spikenard. Some have said this was worth a
year's wage. She began to anoint the feet of Jesus with
this oil.

*Then Mary took a pound of very costly oil of
spikenard, anointed the feet of Jesus, and wiped*

*His feet with her hair. And the house was filled*
*with the fragrance of the oil.*

As she anointed the feet and performed this prophetic act ahead of His death, the aroma filled the
house. Her willingness to take what was so valuable
and pour it on Jesus resulted in the scent touching the
whole house. You can always tell those who have given
the most valuable thing to Jesus. Their brokenness and
willingness to spend and be spent on Jesus changes
the atmosphere. The essence of His presence will come
into these places. It is the testimony of the Holy Spirit
of the life that is being lived. It is a life not necessarily
perfect, but surrendered before Him. These people are
the spikenard being poured over His feet. The aroma of
the anointing released is filling and touching the whole
house/atmosphere. This is why we are cautioned
about not allowing little things to taint the anointing.
Ecclesiastes 10:1 tells us a little foolishness can cause
the anointing and its odor to become polluted.

*Dead flies putrefy the perfumer's ointment,*
*And cause it to give off a foul odor;*
*So does a little folly to one respected for wisdom*
*and honor.*

Those who have been anointed of God must protect
that anointing. The honor and respect that has been gained

because of the anointing must be guarded. If that person becomes prideful, hard, and indifferent to the anointing, it can begin to put off a foul odor rather, not what was intended. These little acts of foolishness cause the anointing to become defiled. Just as dead flies in the anointing oil begin to replace the pleasant aroma with a foul odor.

This was the case with Samson. He was mightily anointed of God as a deliverer. Yet because of weaknesses in his flesh, the anointing of God was tainted. We know he divulged the secret of his anointing to Delilah. The result was the cutting of his hair that took away his supernatural strength. Judges 16:16-20 tells us this sordid story. Samson ended up without the anointing, as weak as other men.

> *And it came to pass, when she pestered him daily with her words and pressed him, so that his soul was vexed to death, that he told her all his heart, and said to her, "No razor has ever come upon my head, for I have been a Nazirite to God from my mother's womb. If I am shaven, then my strength will leave me, and I shall become weak, and be like any other man."*
>
> *When Delilah saw that he had told her all his heart, she sent and called for the lords of the Philistines, saying, "Come up once more, for he has told me all his heart." So the lords of the Philistines came*

*up to her and brought the money in their hand.*
*Then she lulled him to sleep on her knees, and*
*called for a man and had him shave off the seven*
*locks of his head. Then she began to torment him,*
*and his strength left him. And she said, "The*
*Philistines are upon you, Samson!" So he awoke*
*from his sleep, and said, "I will go out as before,*
*at other times, and shake myself free!" But he did*
*not know that the Lord had departed from him.*

Notice that she was unrelenting in discovering the source of his strength. It wasn't his hair, but it was more what his hair represented—his consecrated dedication as a Nazirite to his God. She pestered him daily. This speaks of that thing that will not leave us alone. It attacks us and seeks to erode away our defenses. That temptation. Those words of accusation. The pressure from life. These and other things are after the secret to our strength. They want to snip it away and take from us the anointing on our life. They want to bring us to compromise that will put flies in the ointment.

This happened to Samson. The sad fact is the anointing left him and he didn't know it. He went out and shook himself and didn't know the presence of the Lord was no longer there. May the Lord help us. Even in his statement that *"I will go out as before, at other times, and shake myself free!"* there is a revelation. Instead of living his life in communion with the presence of the Lord, Samson practiced compromise. He would indulge in the flesh, then stir himself back up. As a result of the covenant he had with God, the anointing was always there. However, when the covenant of the Nazirite was broken, the anointing lifted. It was no longer on his life. It wasn't there to stir up anymore. We must learn to live without compromise. Then we will not have to *stir up* the anointing. It will be always resident on our lives. May we remove from the anointing oil the dead little flies. May the anointing on our lives put forth a sweet, fragrant aroma.

## Myrrh

Let's take a look at five ingredients to the anointing oil. The first mentioned is myrrh. The word *myrrh* means "bitter" in the Hebrew. It was one of the principal things used for embalming. It speaks of these bitter places in life where death to self occurs. We all walk through these places. In these places we must find the grace of God. Otherwise, the bitter places will make us bitter people. Hebrews 12:15 lets us know that we *must* discover God's grace in these times of bitterness.

*Looking carefully lest anyone fall short of the grace of God; lest any root of bitterness spring-ing up cause trouble, and by this many become defiled.*

Grace discovered in places of bitterness will not allow us to become bitter. If we allow a root of bitterness to develop, it will poison every other thing, even other people. However, if we allow the healing grace of Jesus to help us and restore our souls, we will receive His anointing from that grace. The grace received in this place of healing will result in new dimensions of His anointing and mantling. Pray this prayer from the Courts of Heaven.

As I stand before Your Courts, Lord Jesus, I bring all my wounds, hurts, and disap-pointments before You. I repent for allowing them to flavor my life. I am sorry for allow-ing these things that have caused me pain to make me angry, bitter, and even hateful. I surrender to You and ask for Your blood to cleanse this away. May Your grace work in my life in the midst of bitterness and hurt. I receive this from Your gracious hand right now. I forgive any and all who have hurt and harmed me. I release them into Your grace. May this be recorded before Your

Courts that this is my heart and desire. May it speaks before Your there and allow me to move into the new mantling of the Lord. In Jesus' Name, amen.


## Cinnamon

The second ingredient of the anointing oil is sweet smelling cinnamon. One of the attributes of cinnamon is that it accents other flavors present. This is what the anointing does. It will empower and embellish the present gifting we already have. Things we already carry will be greatly influenced. An example of this is the rod of Moses that became the Rod of God. This was a stick that Moses had *picked up* on his journey. He probably never dreamed it would be used to bring God's people from captivity. Somewhere along the way, Moses had discovered this stick. He thought it would be a good tool to help shepherd the sheep of his father-in-law. He picked it up and began to use it for that purpose. Exodus 4:1-5 chronicles the encounter where this rod transitioned to the Rod of God.

*Then Moses answered and said, "But suppose they will not believe me or listen to my voice;*

*suppose they say, 'The Lord has not appeared to you.'"*

*So the Lord said to him, "What is that in your hand?"*

*He said, "A rod."*

*And He said, "Cast it on the ground." So he cast it on the ground, and it became a serpent; and Moses fled from it. Then the Lord said to Moses, "Reach out your hand and take it by the tail" (and he reached out his hand and caught it, and it became a rod in his hand), "that they may believe that the Lord God of their fathers, the God of Abraham, the God of Isaac, and the God of Jacob, has appeared to you."*

In other words, the rod he was carrying already was greatly impacted in the presence and the glory of the Lord. With this rod he would divide the Red Sea (see Exod. 14:16). With is rod he would release judgments against Egypt (see Exod. 7:19). He would do many other things with this rod in hand. It would become known as the Rod of God. Exodus 4:20 shows that what had been only a stick in Moses' hand, under the anointing, became the Rod of God.

*Then Moses took his wife and his sons and set them on a donkey, and he returned to the land of Egypt. And Moses took the rod of God in his hand.*

This is a good picture of what can happen under the anointing. What is insignificant can become greatly empowered. This is because the anointing takes our *natural* and adds *super* to it. It becomes the supernatural of God. This is what cinnamon speaks of in the anointing oil. Here is a prayer to pray to accent what we are already carrying from the mantles we receive.

As I come before Your Courts, I ask that the mantling of the Lord would now come on my life. May this mantling release and accent the gifts and abilities I already carry. May they become greatly empowered from the mantles I am receiving from You and Your Courts this day. In Jesus' Name, amen.

## Sweet-Smelling Cane

The next ingredient mentioned is sweet-smelling cane. Cane speaks of the authority of God. The reason *cane* is about authority is recorded in Revelation 12:5.

*She bore a male Child who was to rule all nations
with a rod of iron. And her Child was caught up
to God and His throne.*

Cane and a rod are the same thing. When scripture
speaks of rods, it is talking of authority that has been
imparted are granted. Notice that it is *sweet-smelling*
cane. Sometimes we picture authority as an evil thing.
However, the authority that is in the anointing is a
sweet thing. Paul realized this. He knew his authority
he carried was to be for edification and not destruction. This is according to Second Corinthians 10:8.

*For even if I should boast somewhat more about
our authority, which the Lord gave us for edification and not for your destruction, I shall not be
ashamed.*

Quite often I have watched those who have authority operate more in a destructive way than an edifying
way. Anyone who has been entrusted with the anoint-
ing/mantle from the Lord must use the authority
associated with it rightly. Otherwise, that authority
will not only bring destruction to others, it will ultimately destroy them as well. Jesus speaks of this in
Luke 12:43-46.

*Blessed is that servant whom his master will find
so doing when he comes. Truly, I say to you that*

*he will make him ruler over all that he has. But
if that servant says in his heart, 'My master is
delaying his coming,' and begins to beat the male
and female servants, and to eat and drink and
be drunk, the master of that servant will come
on a day when he is not looking for him, and
at an hour when he is not aware, and will cut
him in two and appoint him his portion with the
unbelievers.*

Anyone granted and entrusted authority who misuses it will be punished by the ultimate authority Himself. If they abuse others from the authority given, live fleshly and sensual lives, they will be punished greatly. It says they will be given a portion with the unbelievers. We must guard our hearts that the authority we are walking in is sweet! We must use it to bless others, not oppress them. This is a part of the mantling of the Lord we have received.

## Cassia

The next ingredient of the anointing oil is cassia. *Cassia* in the Hebrew means "to shrivel, to bend the neck in deference." Clearly this is a reference to humility. However, it is not just a humility toward the Lord but toward others as well. When you *defer* to someone else, you are honoring and setting them before yourself. This is the spirit in which the Lord Himself walked. Philippians 2:1-5 describes the way Jesus walked and the way we are to walk as well.

> *Therefore if there is any consolation in Christ, if any comfort of love, if any fellowship of the Spirit, if any affection and mercy, fulfill my joy by being like-minded, having the same love, being of one accord, of one mind. Let nothing be done through selfish ambition or conceit, but in lowliness of mind let each esteem others better than himself. Let each of you look out not only for his own interests, but also for the interests of others. Let this mind be in you which was also in Christ Jesus.*

We are to esteem other better than ourselves. We are to look out not only for our own interests, but also for the interests of others. This was the mind that was in Jesus. This is deference described. This is one of the ingredients of the anointing oil. Jesus and John the Baptist exemplified this. When Jesus came to be baptized by John, John sought to resist Him. John knew by the Spirit who Jesus was. He was esteemed to be the greater. We see this dialogue in Matthew 3:13-17.

*Then Jesus came from Galilee to John at the Jordan to be baptized by him. And John tried to prevent Him, saying, "I need to be baptized by You, and are You coming to me?"*

*But Jesus answered and said to him, "Permit it to be so now, for thus it is fitting for us to fulfill all righteousness." Then he allowed Him.*

*When He had been baptized, Jesus came up immediately from the water; and behold, the heavens were opened to Him, and He saw the Spirit of God descending like a dove and alighting upon Him. And suddenly a voice came from heaven, saying, "This is My beloved Son, in whom I am well pleased."*

Jesus and John argued over who would get to be the least. When was the last time you saw this happen? Usually people are jockeying for position. Usually they are trying to climb over each other to the top. Yet Jesus and John, at the least, had a conversation over who was going to take the lower place. This would not be the case later on with Jesus' disciples. They would literally contend with each other about who was the greatest. Mark 9:33-35 shows Jesus confronting this spirit of exaltation that was in His disciples.

*Then He came to Capernaum. And when He was in the house He asked them, "What was it you*

*disputed among yourselves on the road?" But
they kept silent, for on the road they had disputed
among themselves who would be the greatest.
And He sat down, called the twelve, and said to
them, "If anyone desires to be first, he shall be
last of all and servant of all."*

Jesus was seeking to get them to understand the need
to have a servant's heart. He knew that to accomplish
what He would leave them to do, they would have to
learn to serve. They would have to walk in the spirit of
deferring to each other. When Jesus and John walked
in this spirit, the heavens opened. The Holy Spirit
descended on Jesus. This is because the Spirit of God
honors this heart of deference and servanthood. It wasn't
until the disciples came to this place of surrender to God
and before each other that the Holy Spirit manifested in
power. Acts 2:1-2 shows that as they were together in
unity and love for each other, the Spirit suddenly came.

*When the Day of Pentecost had fully come, they
were all with one accord in one place. And suddenly there came a sound from heaven, as of a
rushing mighty wind, and it filled the whole
house where they were sitting.*

The word for *one accord* in the Greek is *homothu-
madon*. These words together mean *violent unity*. The

disciples were no longer disputing over who would get to be the greatest. Something had happened in that upper room in those ten days between Jesus' ascension and the outpouring of the Holy Spirit. They had come to a place of genuine care, love, and deference to each other. They no longer were seeking to take the highest place for themselves. They were just tolerating each other. They had come to a place of laying aside ego and even their own interests. They had begun to esteem others better than themselves. Just like when Jesus was baptized, the power of the Holy Spirit came into that house. They were all gloriously baptized in His presence and glory. This one quality seems to be something the Spirit of God is drawn to. If we desire the mantle of the Holy Spirit on our lives, we must let this deference be worked into our lives. Whoever will be great must become the servant of all! Let's pray this prayer.

> As I come before Your Courts, Lord, let it be known that I desire to walk in humility before You and in deference with other people. I am sorry for the places I have insisted on my own rights, desires, and selfish ambitions. Today, let it be recorded that I lay this aside and prefer Your will and the desires of others ahead of myself. Let this same spirit and mind that is in You, Lord, be in me. I ask

that this might be known before You and Your Courts. Lord, allow the mantle and anointing of the Holy Spirit to now come on me as it did Jesus and the disciples. In Jesus' Name. Amen.

## Olive Oil

The last ingredient to be mentioned in the making of the anointing oil is *olive oil*. The making of olive oil requires the crushing of the olive to extract the oil. If we are to be mantled with the anointing of God, we must allow the breaking of the Lord to occur in our life. Anyone who carries the mantle of the Lord will do so because they have been reduced to weakness. We think God is drawn to our strength. The reality is, God is drawn to our weakness and brokenness before Him. Anyone who stands in power in public will have been broken in private. This is why Paul spoke of weakness. Second Corinthians 12:9-10 shows the apostle Paul glorying in his weakness. He explained that his weakness allowed a greater realm of power to rest on him.

> *And He said to me, "My grace is sufficient for you, for My strength is made perfect in weakness." Therefore most gladly I will rather boast*

*in my infirmities, that the power of Christ may rest upon me. Therefore I take pleasure in infirmities, in reproaches, in needs, in persecutions, in distresses, for Christ's sake. For when I am weak, then I am strong.*

What a statement. Paul was explaining that when he was crushed and broken, it allowed a great realm of power to manifest. Anyone who operates in the power, glory, and anointing of the Lord will have been broken in the inner places. This brokenness allows the grace and power of Jesus to be seen. First Corinthians 2:3-4 also shows this principle at work.

*I was with you in weakness, in fear, and in much trembling. And my speech and my preaching were not with persuasive words of human wisdom, but in demonstration of the Spirit and of power.*

Notice that Paul in the flesh had no confidence. He was in a place of absolute dependence on the Lord. Therefore, the ministry flowed forth not with man's wisdom, but in the power of God. If we are to be mantled of the Lord, we must allow the breaking of God to bring us to this place. This doesn't mean bad things are going to happen to us. It means that in His presence all stubbornness and self-will are consumed. We come to a position of surrender in the depths of our spirit. This is what happened to Moses. Moses understood he was to be a deliverer of his people from Egypt. However, he tried to do it from his own strength. In Acts 7:23-25 Stephen, in speaking before the Jewish leaders, cited Moses and his efforts in the flesh to deliver God's people.

> *Now when he was forty years old, it came into his heart to visit his brethren, the children of Israel. And seeing one of them suffer wrong, he defended and avenged him who was oppressed, and struck down the Egyptian. For he supposed that his brethren would have understood that God would deliver them by his hand, but they did not understand.*

Moses then spent the next 40 years exiled in the backside of the desert. God emptied him of self in this time. Then He appeared to him and commissioned him from His strength. This is a process we all must go through. If we are to be mantled by God, we will first be brought to a weakness. We will have no confidence in the flesh, but know that only through His power can we see His work done. Let's petition the Courts of Heaven for this.

> As I come before Your Courts, Lord, I surrender all my own efforts, power, and abilities.

I yield to You and proclaim that only by Your empowerment can the work be done. I need You! Let me have no confidence in the flesh, but only in Your Spirit. I declare I am weak, but You are strong. I draw from Your strength even in the midst of my weakness. I learn to take pleasure in weakness, for in this place I discover Your strength. Would You allow this to be known before Your Courts? Would You let it be recorded and allow the mantle of God to now come in me in this place of weakness? In Jesus' Name, amen.

CHAPTER 8

# CARRYING MANTLES

O nce we have been entrusted with a mantle from heaven, we must carry it and steward it well. This is where the enemy, the devil, can find places to accuse us. Our endeavor should be to be like Jesus. Remember that He said the devil had come looking but had found no place to accuse Him. We see this in John 14:30.

> *I will no longer talk much with you, for the ruler of this world is coming, and he has nothing in Me.*

There were no grounds for a Court case against Jesus. He had lived His life in such a way that the devil could bring no word against Him. If we have been guilty of exploiting the anointing for personal gain, the devil will use this to deny us mantles. As we cry for the mantling of the Lord, he will raise a case against us to prohibit this. We can see some of the things he will use in Exodus 30:30-33. These were guidelines the

Lord gave concerning the carrying of the anointing/ mantles.

> And you shall anoint Aaron and his sons, and consecrate them, that they may minister to Me as priests.
>
> And you shall speak to the children of Israel, saying: "This shall be a holy anointing oil to Me throughout your generations. It shall not be poured on man's flesh; nor shall you make any other like it, according to its composition. It is holy, and it shall be holy to you. Whoever compounds any like it, or whoever puts any of it on an outsider, shall be cut off from his people."

There are six guidelines here to stewarding the anointing of the Lord. If we have been guilty of violating any of these, the devil will bring accusation against us from them. These can be used to deny us a greater mantling and glory on our lives.

## For the Lord

The first principle of the anointing is *it is for the Lord*. Notice that Aaron and his sons were anointed to minister to God as priests. The anointing was for the purpose of serving the Lord acceptably. We cannot serve God correctly or successfully without the anointing. Hebrews 12:28 tells us that we must have the spirit of grace on us. Without His empowerment, we cannot serve Him and be accepted.

> *Therefore, since we are receiving a kingdom which cannot be shaken, let us have grace, by which we may serve God acceptably with reverence and godly fear.*

It is His anointing that empowers us for service. However, the anointing isn't given to make us famous or rich. The anointing is given for the purpose of fulfilling His purpose. This is one of the main objections that satan brings against us as we contend to carry new mantles. We must allow the purification of our motives. We see this happening in Acts 8:17-23. Simon the sorcerer had seemingly been converted as Philip ministered in Samaria. The apostles had come to administer the Holy Spirit into the new believers' lives.

> *Then they laid hands on them, and they received the Holy Spirit.*
>
> *And when Simon saw that through the laying on of the apostles' hands the Holy Spirit was given, he offered them money, saying, "Give me*

*this power also, that anyone on whom I lay hands
may receive the Holy Spirit."*

*But Peter said to him, "Your money perish with
you, because you thought that the gift of God
could be purchased with money! You have neither
part nor portion in this matter, for your heart is
not right in the sight of God. Repent therefore of
this your wickedness, and pray God if perhaps
the thought of your heart may be forgiven you.
For I see that you are poisoned by bitterness and
bound by iniquity."*

Simon had been held in high esteem by the people
prior to this great move of God. As people began to
turn to the Lord, they no longer would have regarded
him. Even though he had believed and was baptized,
it was difficult for him to lose this place in the culture
he had occupied. When he saw the apostles moving
in power, he couldn't contain himself. He had to have
that power that he might reestablish himself in the eyes
of the people. He wanted what the apostles carried but
for the wrong reason. His motives were corrupt.

Peter's exhortation to him was very strong. He told
him he couldn't *buy* this power. Many today still think
that the mantles of the Holy Spirit are for sale. Some
give offerings from this standpoint. We know that we
worship the Lord with our offerings and bring them

before Him in adoration of who He is. However, some would think God owes them something because of an offering they have given. This is completely wrong. Our offerings can and should be statements of faith and adoration toward God. However, He does not owe us something because we gave. We must allow the Lord to purify our heart that we might bring offerings of righteousness to Him (see Mal. 3:3). These offerings speak before His Courts on our behalf as we allow this cleansing to take place.

Simon was trying to buy the anointing/mantle. People try to buy in other ways. They think that all the time they spend in prayer will impress God so He will give them a mantle. Or maybe because they have confessed the Word diligently, they will be granted one. Anything that slips over into a works mentality to get something from God will not succeed. Romans 4:1-4 gives us great insight into escaping this mentality.

> *What then shall we say that Abraham our father has found according to the flesh? For if Abraham was justified by works, he has something to boast about, but not before God. For what does the Scripture say? "Abraham believed God, and it was accounted to him for righteousness." Now to him who works, the wages are not counted as grace but as debt.*

Abraham discovered something as he journeyed with God. He found out that God doesn't respond to our religious works. We are not to try and impress Him. To seek to impress God with our works is to make Him our debtor. In other words, if I pray, fast, go to church, worship, give, and other activities, God owes me. It is not of works but of grace. It is the goodness and kindness of the Lord that responds to my reaching out to Him in faith. It is not my religious activities but my heart to seek Him that pleases Him.It is so easy to slip into a mindset of *buying* something from the Lord. We must repent of this. The anointing isn't for sale at any price. We must want it for the right reasons. That reason is to serve God and His purposes. This is what God said to Moses: "Anoint Aaron and his sons that they may minister to *Me* as priests." Lord, may we have the anointing and mantle that we might serve You acceptably. Let's bring this issue of motives before the Courts of Heaven.

> As I come before Your Courts, Lord, I acknowledge my wrong motives for the anointing. Only You, Lord, can change my heart. I ask that there might be a purifying of my heart. Let me desire the mantles of God, but for the right reasons. Forgive my desiring the powers of God in the past that I might be known, famous, and even wealthy

because of it. I say before You that this is wickedness before You and I repent. Allow a pure, right heart to be in me. Let me desire the anointing and mantles of God that Your purposes might be served. Let it be recorded before Your Courts that I am requesting this today. I love You, Lord, and want to be holy before You. In Jesus' Name, amen.

## Generational

The next guideline and principle of stewarding the anointing is it must be *generational.* We are told that this anointing oil is to be considered holy for generations. The nature of the anointing is that it can be passed from generation to generation. In fact, this in one of the main ways that the kingdom of God expands from generation to generation. Daniel 4:3 tells us that the dominion of the kingdom of God is a generational issue.

> *How great are His signs,*
> *And how mighty His wonders!*
> *His kingdom is an everlasting kingdom,*
> *And His dominion is from generation to*
> *generation.*

When the Bible speaks of the dominion of His kingdom, it is declaring the functional rule of God in the earth. This is a result of the anointing being passed from generation to generation. The problem is that many anointings have not been stewarded and passed to succeeding generations. They ceased to operate when the ones who carried them died. This is why there is a room in heaven where mantles are stored. It is because they were never transmitted to the coming generations. This is primarily because those who carried the mantles never raised sons and daughters. They were content to carry and minister from the mantle but not produce sons and daughters who would carry it to the next level.

As mantles move from generation to generation, they will not just stay the same. They should accelerate and become more powerful. However, for this to happen sons and daughters must be raised to whom the mantles can be imparted. We know that Paul imparted to Timothy, his spiritual son. We know Moses gave to Joshua some of his authority and wisdom. We also know Elijah gave the mantle to Elisha. All of these were father-and-son relationships that allowed this impartation.

There are two reasons why this generational transmission hasn't occurred. One is that men and women of God greatly mantled by the Lord didn't understand the need for sons and daughters. They saw themselves as a phenomenon for their generation alone. This is one of the reasons that some of the mantles in my prophet friend's dream had only one name written on the collar. It was carried by one alone because there was never an effort to raise sons and daughters.

The other reason is that there have been few *true* sons and daughters in the faith. It is quite an obligation to walk as a son or daughter of a man or woman of God. When you walk in this level of commitment, you see the good, bad, and ugly. You must be one who is not easily turned aside by the failure of humanity. I'm not talking about gross sin of immorality or ethics. These things cannot be tolerated. However, the personality clashes, rudeness, and offenses that arise have to be overcome.

Let me tell you of a situation I experienced while being raised by a true spiritual father. I began this journey along with several others who were being fathered by this man. As far as I know, out of all those who began only two of us made it through. All the others became offended, failed to endure, and simply bailed out. There were times as I was being trained when my spiritual father would withdraw himself from me. I wondered at the time if it was my imagination, or if it was really happening. It seemed as if he would get distant and be unaccepting of me.

Of course, as he was one I esteemed as my father in the faith, I desperately wanted his approval. This man was in no way emotional or given to moodiness. This wasn't the case. I felt in these moments that I had displeased him and couldn't be accepted. This forced me to find my approval in God. It caused me to go to prayer more deeply and have the Lord confirm me rather than this human person. It would seem that this coldness would last for a season, then the communion I so enjoyed would be restored. This happened several times in the process of my tutoring for ministry and life.

After years of walking intimately with the man, I was sent out to lead my own church. Because the city I was in was close to where my father in the faith operated, I would go back occasionally to see him. As I dropped in one day, the secretary, whom I knew very well, said I had just missed him. She then began to tell me that my father in the faith had divulged something to her about me. She told me that he said there were times when I was being raised up that he would withdraw himself from me. My first thought was, *So it wasn't my imagination.* She went on to say that he said the reason he did this was to teach me to handle rejection. This statement was then made. He said, *"If Robert can't handle rejection, Robert can't be in the ministry."* What a statement and what a wise man to prepare a son for ministry.

Of course, he was exactly right. There can be much rejection in ministry. If we don't know how to find acceptance and approval from the Lord Himself, it will destroy us. However, if we know the approval of God we can weather any storm of rejection. What if I had of bailed out when the coldness came? What if I had gotten offended and reacted? I would have lost the right to be a son and to receive the impartation. The anointing is generational. We must have men and women of God who are willing to father and mother. We also must have sons and daughters who will pay the price to be true sons and daughters as well. This will allow the generational aspect of the anointing to be transmitted and received. Here is a prayer from the Courts of Heaven to deal with anything the devil is using in this area.

> As I come before Your Courts, Lord, I repent of any place I have short-circuited Your plan for generational transmission of the anointing. Lord, forgive me for being offended and disconnecting from any father or mother you have set in my life. I ask that the blood would speak for me and cleanse this away. Also, Lord, as a father or mother please allow me to walk in such a way that any and every anointing/mantle might be imparted. I'm asking this in Jesus' Name, amen.

## Not on Flesh

The third guideline and principle for stewarding the anointing is that it cannot be put on flesh. We are never to anoint or expect flesh to be anointed. We cannot live fleshly lives given to the desires of our flesh and expect to be anointed. This is one of the main areas of consecration for many of us. Learning to say no to our flesh and its desires and appetites is a big part of our lives as believers. In today's world of a hyper-grace message, this understanding is greatly needed. The present day message of grace is taught in such a way that it gives license to the fulfilling of the lusts of the flesh. This is what we are warned about in Jude 4.

> *For certain men have crept in unnoticed, who long ago were marked out for this condemnation, ungodly men, who turn the grace of our God into lewdness and deny the only Lord God and our Lord Jesus Christ.*

These are those who have warped and perverted the true grace of our God. They teach that you can live any way you desire and it's okay with God. This scripture, however, says these are marked for judgment and are denying the real Lord Jesus Christ. I don't want to be number among these. Paul would further espouse that we should never adopt the attitude that it's okay to sin. Romans 6:1-2 says that everything that is new in us from our new birth screams against this idea.

> *What shall we say then? Shall we continue in sin that grace may abound? Certainly not! How shall we who died to sin live any longer in it?*

Here we are given the key to overcoming fleshly living. Remember that the anointing can never be placed on flesh. We must know that when Jesus died on the cross, He didn't just die for us. We also died with Him. This means the old nature that wants to do wrong and lusts after things of the flesh died at the cross with Jesus. We are told in Romans 6:11 that we are to esteem this to be so. We are to believe by faith this spiritual reality is active in our lives.

> *Likewise you also, reckon yourselves to be dead indeed to sin, but alive to God in Christ Jesus our Lord.*

This means that I, by faith, set in place the accomplishments of Jesus on my behalf from the cross. The old nature that loves to live in the flesh has died with Him on the cross. This is imperative for us to live free from fleshly living. Second Corinthians 7:1 tells us what our response should be to this.

*Therefore, having these promises, beloved, let us cleanse ourselves from all filthiness of the flesh and spirit, perfecting holiness in the fear of God.*

Notice we are told that we should *cleanse ourselves.* In other words, we take up the authority we have been granted and we start walking in a new way. Of course, the Holy Spirit is there to empower us. However, it is a choice we make based on all that Jesus has provided for us. We are empowered to live this clean and holy life before Him. This will allow us to be anointed with fresh oil. With all this said, we live in an unclean world. As we walk in it, there will be defilements that want to attach themselves to us. This means we must *wash* regularly. Jesus actually spoke of this when He washed the disciples' feet in John 13:10. When Peter resisted the idea of Jesus washing his feet, Jesus let him know that he wouldn't be esteemed as belonging to Him without it. Peter then reversed course and said, "Then wash all of me." Jesus made this powerful statement at this point.

*Jesus said to him, "He who is bathed needs only to wash his feet, but is completely clean; and you are clean, but not all of you."*

Jesus corrected Peter and let him know that when you are *bathed* or saved/born again you are clean.

However, as you walk through the uncleanness of this world, dirt is going to get on you. This means you need to wash your feet on a regular basis. This keeps the sin off of you and stops the hardness of heart from occurring. We can see this idea referred to when Paul instructed Timothy in Second Timothy 3:6-7. Paul admonished that there were unscrupulous people who would sway the hearts of those who hadn't been washed regularly.

> *For of this sort are those who creep into households and make captives of gullible women loaded down with sins, led away by various lusts, always learning and never able to come to the knowledge of the truth.*

Notice that the thing that allowed the deception was they were *loaded down with sin*. When we do not wash and experience cleansing on a regular basis, sin begins to cake on us. It will cause us to compromise and not walk before the Lord in a right way. We need the daily washing of the Lord. We need the washing of the word (see Eph. 5:26). We need the washing of His presence. We need the washing of right and good fellowship. All of this and other ways can keep us from sin and defiling the flesh. This will cause us to walk in the anointing and power of the Holy Spirit. Here's a prayer from the Courts of Heaven to break the power of the flesh.

As I come before Your Courts, Lord, I acknowledge my struggle with the flesh. Lord, I want to live holy. I want to be clean before You. Would You allow every defilement to be purged by Your blood? Let Your blood speak for me and cause the cleansing of the Lord to purify any defilement in my conscience. I declare before Your Courts that I have received Your new nature into my life. I say that my old nature has died with You at the cross. I reckon it to be so now. Let every defilement of the flesh now be removed far from me in Jesus' Name. Would You now allow Your presence anointing oil/mantle come on my life? Let the empowerment of Your Spirit be mine that Your purposes might be done in the earth. In Jesus' Name, amen.

## No Substitutions

Another guideline and principle for stewarding the anointing is never try to duplicate or substitute something for the anointing. As we saw in Exodus 30:32, it was a grave sin to fabricate something to operate in the place of the real anointing.

*It shall not be poured on man's flesh; nor shall
you make any other like it, according to its composition. It is holy, and it shall be holy to you.*

I am sad to say that I have witnessed this many
times. Either through ignorance or on purpose, people have sought to substitute something for the real
anointing. They have spoken of the presence of God
that was present when it was just lively music. They
have said the glory was present when it was just a soft,
melancholy atmosphere that had been created. The fact
is that many people say these things because they have
no awareness of the real anointing of God. They've
never really tasted of the glory and presence of God.
As a result, they think the substitute is the real.I have
been in so many services where the singing went on
for so long with no real presence of God that could be
perceived. It is very laborious and wearisome. Yet the
leader would get up and declare what a glory of God
was present. I would sit there thinking either I'm a rep-
robate and don't know anything or someone is greatly
mistaken. So much of this is because we have been
inundated with things called the anointing that are not
the anointing. We must repent for creating substitutes
for the real anointing oil of God. We must repent of
the hype we have propagated as the anointing of God.
I believe these sins are grievous because they end up
belittling the real anointing of the Lord. This is what

has happened in the church. Our hype that we have created, when there was nothing present, has been used by the devil. He whispers in people's ears that it is all just a show. We are told of this in Jude 12.

> *These are spots in your love feasts, while they feast with you without fear, serving only themselves. They are clouds without water, carried about by the winds; late autumn trees without fruit, twice dead, pulled up by the roots.*

I am not saying that all this verse applies to most. Many are sincere; they've just never known the real presence, power, and anointing of God. However, some of the verse does apply. They do espouse great glory is present. They are clouds without water. They make great boasts about the glory of God, yet in reality there is nothing. They are, in fact, clouds that promise rain, but there is no moisture/anointing. We must repent for being clouds without rain and, as Second Peter 2:17 declares, wells without water.

> *These are wells without water, clouds carried by a tempest, for whom is reserved the blackness of darkness forever.*

Again, for many the entirety of this verse is not applicable. However, we have been not only clouds without rain, but also wells with water. We have promised that if people would just draw, there would be the water and presence of the Holy Spirit. Yet when it was all said and done, there was nothing but dry barrenness at the bottom of the well. All of this speaks of promising something but nothing happening. This is because we are substituting something for the anointing. If we want the new mantles of God, for this we must repent!

The reason people hype things up and call it the anointing is because they will not pay the price for the real glory. They have chosen to adopt lifestyles that will not allow the mantles of God to be deposited. There is a cost to living in and functioning from the anointing of the Lord. It is the cost of self-sacrifice, holiness, seeking God, and sleepless times of prayer. The Lord will honor us with His wonderful presence when the cost is paid. We will not have to revert to substituting things for the real anointing of God. I believe Jesus spoke of this in John 5:44. He speaks of the *honor* that comes from the Lord. I believe this is the anointing and mantle of God that we carry.

> *How can you believe, who receive honor from one another, and do not seek the honor that comes from the only God?*

The honor of God is the manifest glory of God. When God chooses to move through His anointing on our life, this is His honor. Jesus spoke of it further in John 8:54.

> *Jesus answered, "If I honor Myself, My honor is nothing. It is My Father who honors Me, of whom you say that He is your God."*

When manifestations of the anointing are seen through our lives, it is God verifying that we are His. This is the real honor of the Lord. It is very much as Moses going into the tabernacle of meeting and the glory coming down on it. We see this in Exodus 33:8-11. God honored Moses in the sight of the people by coming down to meet with him.

> *So it was, whenever Moses went out to the tabernacle, that all the people rose, and each man stood at his tent door and watched Moses until he had gone into the tabernacle. And it came to pass, when Moses entered the tabernacle, that the pillar of cloud descended and stood at the door of the tabernacle, and the Lord talked with Moses. All the people saw the pillar of cloud standing at the tabernacle door, and all the people rose and worshiped, each man in his tent door. So the Lord spoke to Moses face to face, as a man speaks to his friend. And he would return to the camp, but his*

*servant Joshua the son of Nun, a young man, did
not depart from the tabernacle.*

There are times when people who know God begin
to pray. In essence, the same thing occurs as happens
here. Their prayer actually causes the presence, anointing, and glory of God to come. It is the Lord coming
down to meet with them as He came to meet with
Moses. He comes to speak with us as His friend in
these moments. This is the honor of God. There has
been a price paid to carry the true anointing of His
Spirit. His presence is the honor of that person! We
must desire and pursue this honor above all else. With
it there will be no need for a substitute. Let's pray this
prayer before His Courts.

> As I come before Your Courts, Lord, I repent
> for the places I have substituted hype, music,
> and even gifts for the real anointing of God.
> Forgive me for not paying the price to walk
> in Your glory and presence. I ask that every
> claim of the devil of mis-stewarding the
> anointing in this way would be dismissed.
> Let Your precious blood now speak for me,
> I pray. I repent for seeking the honor of man
> more than the honor of God. I pray that
> this might be recorded and regarded before
> Your Courts. Let this repentance speak on

my behalf that I might qualify for the new mantles of the Lord. In Jesus' Name, amen.

## Covenant People

The last thing the anointing of God testifies of is a *covenant people*. We are told that the anointing was not to be placed on strangers or those outside of covenant with the Lord. Exodus 30:33 reflects this.

> *Whoever compounds any like it, or whoever puts any of it on an outsider, shall be cut off from his people.*

An outsider spoke of one who was not a part of Israel and had not been circumcised. The anointing oil is only for people in covenant with God. This is why we are told in Romans 8:16 that His spirit testifies that we belong to Him.

> *The Spirit Himself bears witness with our spirit that we are children of God.*

We do not base our eternal security on a doctrine, a man's opinion, or a favorite Bible teacher. Our eternal security is based on the witness of the Holy Spirit in our hearts. He settles, secures, sanctifies, and confirms those who have been purchased by the blood of the Lamb. Those who really belong to Jesus, the Holy Spirit anoints. This is why we are told Second Corinthians 1:21-22 that we have the earnest or down payment of the Holy Spirit as His blood-bought saints.

> *Now He who establishes us with you in Christ and has anointed us is God, who also has sealed us and given us the Spirit in our hearts as a guarantee.*

The Spirit in our hearts is the signal that we are His. This is why the anointing oil was to only go on covenant people. It was to be a consistent type that when we have the Spirit, it is because we belong to Him. As long as the Holy Spirit is testifying to us that we are the Lord's, there is great peace and confidence with God. We should thank the Lord in the Courts of Heaven and acknowledge this great assurance.

> As I stand in the Courts of Heaven, thank You, Lord, for the Person of the Holy Spirit who testifies that I am Yours. May He take more and more of my life in consecration to You. Thank You that the Spirit is witnessing and silencing every fear. His testimony that I am saved, born again, and redeemed settles every concern I have. You are my God and

my King. I belong to You. Let it be recorded that this is my statement and the statement of the Holy Spirit before Your presence. In Jesus' Name, amen.

# CHAPTER 9

# MANTLES AND IMPARTATION

The whole idea of impartation always excites me. I love the idea that something spiritual can be transmitted into my life. The concept that through hands, word, prophecy, and atmospheres I can catch something from another is quite profound. We have all probably heard the statement that the anointing is more *caught* than *taught*. This is absolutely true. However, it takes a spirit of faith to catch the anointing and mantles. Clearly Elisha caught something that was released by Elijah. This was a place of impartation. Yet there are others in scripture who caught the anointing/mantles of God. We will look at the four realms of impartation that I mentioned. Again, they are hands, word, prophecy, and atmospheres. Through any or all of these realms impartation can take place. As we look at impartation of mantles, Paul expressed his desire to impact the Romans through this idea. Romans 1:11

shows him desiring to be with them so that he could impart spiritual gifts.

*For I long to see you, that I may impart to you some spiritual gift, so that you may be established.*

There are several things concerning impartation that stand out in this scripture. First of all, Paul seems very certain that if he can physically be among them, they will receive a spiritual gift. The word spiritual is the Greek word pneumatikos. It means "a spirit, divinely supernatural." Paul was declaring that when he would be among them, there would be a supernatural element that would be passed from him to them. The word gift is the Greek word charisma. This word means "an endowment, a qualification, a miraculous faculty." Clearly Paul was letting it be known that when he saw these believers there would be a deposit of supernatural power. That which they didn't presently carry, they would then possess.

This scripture then declares it is so they can be established. This word is sterizo. It means "to turn resolutely in a certain direction." The impartation that Paul yearns to give them will give them new direction in life. It will not just be a gift they can operate in; it will set their course. This is the power of an impartation. When impartation of mantles occurs, it starts changing us and perhaps the direction we are going.

Usually with mantles go assignments. The mantle we receive in impartation will unleash a driving force in our lives. It will give us a determination to fulfill the assignments that the mantle is for. It can change the way we think and our outlook on life. We have been resolutely turned in a certain direction.

One of the best places we can see impartation is in the life of Timothy. Paul consistently urged Timothy to steward properly what he had through impartation. Second Timothy 1:6 tells us that there were certain giftings in Timothy because of impartation.

> *Therefore I remind you to stir up the gift of God which is in you through the laying on of my hands.*

Paul was exhorting Timothy to be faithful with what had been given him through impartation. He was to *stir up* that gifting. This word *stir* means to *rekindle.* It also has the idea of "a living thing and an animal or beast." Timothy had living within him a powerful thing from the Spirit of the Lord. However, he had to stimulate and provoke that which was in him. He could not let it just lie dormant. Many people have been given gifts through impartation. However, they have allow that which is in them to go to sleep. It is time to stir up that which is in us and use it for the kingdom of God. I believe this is what the prophet did when he raised the widow's son back to life. Remember in Second Kings 4:33-35:

> *He went in therefore, shut the door behind the two of them, and prayed to the Lord. And he went up and lay on the child, and put his mouth on his mouth, his eyes on his eyes, and his hands on his hands; and he stretched himself out on the child, and the flesh of the child became warm. He returned and walked back and forth in the house, and again went up and stretched himself out on him; then the child sneezed seven times, and the child opened his eyes.*

We see Elisha resurrecting this boy. It has always stood out to me the process that was used to bring life back to this dead child.

Notice that the prophet prayed to the Lord. He then stretched himself on the child. The child's flesh became warm. Then he *walked back and forth* in the house. This is where he was *stirring up* what was in him. One of the ways we stir up the gifting of God in us is through praying in tongues and worship. As we worship and pray in tongues what is in us is energized and activated. The gifting and life of God begin to flow. This is what we are told in Jude 20. Through praying in the Spirit our faith begins to ignite and soar.

*But you, beloved, building yourselves up on your
most holy faith, praying in the Holy Spirit.*

As we worship and pray in the Holy Spirit, in
tongues, there can be a rush of faith that erupts in our
spirit. Even though this is before the New Testament
arrival of the Holy Spirit, there was something in the
prophet that needed to arise. As he walked back and
forth in the house and stirred himself up, what was in
him was ready to bring life into this boy. The prophet
understood that the resurrection life that was in him
had to be imparted to the dead child.

To fully comprehend this, we must understand how
things work in the spirit world. Most people pray *ricochet prayers.* In other words, they stand in earth and
appeal to God in heaven to touch something in earth.
This is not New Testament order. Jesus taught His disciples to pray differently than this. He taught them to
pray *drawing and imparting prayers.* Instead of bounc-
ing a prayer off God and asking Him to do something,
Jesus told us to do it ourselves! Matthew 10:7-8 shows
Jesus instructing His disciples to impart it themselves.

*And as you go, preach, saying, "The kingdom of
heaven is at hand." Heal the sick, cleanse the lep-
ers, raise the dead, cast out demons. Freely you
have received, freely give.*

Notice they were commissioned to give freely because they had received freely. Nowhere in these scriptures do we see Jesus saying to ask God to do anything. He tells them to do it themselves with what they have received. In other words, they have been imparted to, now they are to impart. This is why Peter spoke to the lame man in the Gate Beautiful the way he did. In Acts 3:4-8 we see this miracle on this crippled man.

> *And fixing his eyes on him, with John, Peter said, "Look at us." So he gave them his attention, expecting to receive something from them. Then Peter said, "Silver and gold I do not have, but what I do have I give you: In the name of Jesus Christ of Nazareth, rise up and walk." And he took him by the right hand and lifted him up, and immediately his feet and ankle bones received strength. So he, leaping up, stood and walked and entered the temple with them – walking, leaping, and praising God.*

Peter doesn't ricochet a prayer off God or try to convince God to do something. He literally declares, *"What is in me, I give to you."* This man was healed because the impartation of life that was in Peter went into him. This is the lesson that God also had to teach Moses. In Exodus 14:13-16 and then in verse 21, we see the Red Sea being divided. Yet God had to stop Moses from asking Him to do it, and use what God had put already into Moses' hand.

> *And Moses said to the people, "Do not be afraid. Stand still, and see the salvation of the Lord, which He will accomplish for you today. For the Egyptians whom you see today, you shall see again no more forever. The Lord will fight for you, and you shall hold your peace."*
>
> *And the Lord said to Moses, "Why do you cry to Me? Tell the children of Israel to go forward. But lift up your rod, and stretch out your hand over the sea and divide it. And the children of Israel shall go on dry ground through the midst of the sea."*
>
> *...Then Moses stretched out his hand over the sea; and the Lord caused the sea to go back by a strong east wind all that night, and made the sea into dry land, and the waters were divided.*

Moses at first asked the Lord to do something. Yet the Lord told Moses two things. First, make the people move forward. Moving forward was an act of faith. In actuality, there was no place to go. The Red Sea was blocking their progress and deliverance. Yet when they moved forward, it was a simple act of faith and belief in God. We must know there are some things that will never happen for us until we take a step of faith and move forward. It could be making that phone call, sending that email, texting that person, applying for that job, asking for that date. Even when there seems to be no way, as we move forward God rewards these simple small steps. Our simple steps of faith can unlock great moves of God.

God also had to get Moses out of the ricochet prayer mode. He literally said, *"Why are you crying to Me?"* In other words, "*I have put into your hand what you need to divide this water and see deliverance. Quit asking Me to do it, and do it yourself!"* As Moses stretched the rod in his hand over the sea, the wind started to blow and the sea was parted. It says that God caused it in response to Moses using what was in his hand. From a New Testament perspective, it wasn't the God on the Throne of Heaven who did it; it was the God who lives within. Colossians 1:27 tells us that the hope of glory is the revelation of Christ in us. He is not just the God who reigns from heaven. He is the God who rules in and from our hearts through the Holy Spirit.

> *To them God willed to make known what are the riches of the glory of this mystery among the Gentiles: which is Christ in you, the hope of glory.*

When we understand impartation, these are things to be considered. This was what was occurring when

Elisha raised the dead child up. He was taking what was inside of him and using it to bring life back to this boy.

It says he *stretched* himself over the child. As someone once told me, a grown man doesn't have to stretch himself to cover a boy in the natural. The *stretching* was in the spirit realm. This prophet was stirring himself up and the Spirit who dwelt in him. He was imparting life into this boy. The second time he stretched himself, the impartation of resurrection life brought the boy back to life. We are told that the same power that raised Jesus from the dead lives in us. Ephesians 3:20 lets us know about this power in us.

> *Now to Him who is able to do exceedingly abundantly above all that we ask or think, according to the power that works in us.*

This is quite a phenomenal scripture. God is able to do so much more than we can imagine—not from His power in heaven, but from the power that is in us. In other words, as we learn to use this power, we can see unthinkable things happen in and through our lives. This is the power of impartation. There are definite times when we are to take what lives in us and change life on the planet. May the same power that created the world and raised Jesus from the dead now flow in us and through us to others.

Lord, as we come before Your Courts, we repent for praying ricochet prayers and not functioning in the realms of impartation. Help us, Lord, to recognize who we are in You and to take that place with great boldness. May we not only receive the impartation of mantles, but may we also give them as we recognize who and what lives in us. We repent for any and all agreements with the religious spirit that would sabotage Your purposes through us. Help us, Lord, to receive mantles through impartation and to steward them correctly. Let it be recorded that this is our request before Your Courts this day. Lord, let the impartation of mantles be our portion in Jesus' Name, amen.

# Chapter 10

# FOUR MEANS OF IMPARTATION

As we continue to consider receiving mantles through impartation, we should know there are at least four means to this impartation. We have mentioned them in the last chapter. They are hands, words, prophecy, and atmospheres. We will talk of these in this chapter. First let me finish my thought of how Timothy's life course was set through impartation. As we saw before, Timothy received impartation from Paul and was urged to stir up what he had received. Timothy also received impartation through a group of elders as well. First Timothy 4:14 gives us this insight.

> *Do not neglect the gift that is in you, which was given to you by prophecy with the laying on of the hands of the eldership.*

This was most likely when Timothy was ordained into ministry and/or set into his function. I myself have received great impartation through the hands of eldership. Years ago, as I was being ordained into ministry it was through a group of elders and leaders. They were actually referred to as a prophetic presbytery. Up until this time, ordination had been very simple and formal. Maybe there were a few questions asked of those being ordained and then some simple prayers prayed. It was very formal and not much spirituality to it. However, by the time of my ordination there had been much more revelation garnered. We now understood that ordination should be a time of impartation. Therefore, this group of prophetic elders was gathered to lay hands on me and prophesy. This was to launch me into the ministry that God had called me to. It wasn't just a formality; it was to be life-changing.

I remember to this day several of the words spoken over me that night. Those prophetic words carried grace and power with them into my destiny and future. Let me just mention a couple of them. The first one was a word that told me not to worry about the identity of my ministry. In other words, I wasn't to be concerned with whether I was an apostle, prophet, evangelist, pastor, or teacher. The word went on to say that I would find myself in varying situations. In each situation, whatever was needed, God would do that through me. In those days, we really didn't have an understanding of the apostolic. I now look back and realize this person who prophesied this was actually declaring the function of an apostle. What he described in his prophecy was apostolic ministry. I can say looking back now after almost 40 years of ministry that his word was true. I have functioned this way and in all five areas at given times. The grace that was imparted to me in that time of ordaining has worked in my life to produce this.

The second word that has resonated during all this time was that no matter what success and influence I was allowed, I was always to remain little in my own eyes. The man prophesied that this was the life of Saul, the first king of Israel. In First Samuel 15:17 we see this recorded.

> *So Samuel said, "When you were little in your own eyes, were you not head of the tribes of Israel? And did not the Lord anoint you king over Israel?"*

Saul started off very humble and in great dependence on God. As he took the position of king from the hand of the Lord, arrogance and pride slipped in. It resulted in his disobedience and his destruction. This prophetic elder was warning me that I must stay small in my own sight. This has been something that I have endeavored to do. However, I believe there was a grace imparted to me from that word that has empowered me. As a result of this grace I have been compelled to walk in a way of humility and surrender before God and men.

In the word given to Timothy, Paul told him to not neglect what was imparted to him through the eldership. It seems that Timothy had a tendency toward timidity and shyness. This caused him to be reluctant in the operation of gifting he had received through impartation. Remember that Paul sought to pull him out of fear in Second Timothy 1:7.

> *For God has not given us a spirit of fear, but of*
> *power and of love and of a sound mind.*

This word *fear* means timidity. Timidity is a fear of man. Timothy allow the intimidation of people and the fear of what they thought to cripple his function. This caused him to neglect the gift given to him through impartation. He let the feelings and ideas of people overwhelm him being faithful with the gift/mantle on his life. We are told that the fear of man is a snare in Proverbs 29:25.

> *The fear of man brings a snare,*
> *But whoever trusts in the Lord shall be safe.*

This word *snare* is the Hebrew word *mowqesh*. It means "a hook in the nose or a noose." When we fear people, they can lead us around by the nose. They are in control of our life. This fear must be broken. This is what caused Timothy to neglect the operation of the gift he had received through impartation. I know it is hard for people to believe, but by nature I am a bashful and timid person. In fact, my wife tells that when we were 16 years old and dating, I would not even order my food in the restaurant. I was so timid I wouldn't talk to the waiter or waitress. Mary would order it for me. This is a major problem for someone called to ministry and especially public speaking. Many opportunities would have passed me by if I hadn't of overcome this handicap. One of the things that propelled me past this shyness was the mantle/anointing I received. Even though I was very reluctant in public, when the anointing would come the fear would break. This is what happened with the disciples of old. These same men who hid for fear of the Jews after Jesus' crucifixion were bold and empowered after the anointing of the Holy Spirit came. Acts 4:13 says that the religious leaders were astonished at the boldness of these men who would have otherwise trembled in their presence.

> *Now when they saw the boldness of Peter and John, and perceived that they were uneducated and untrained men, they marveled. And they realized that they had been with Jesus.*

As ignorant and untrained men, they should have been petrified before these men who had the power to do them much harm. However, because they had been with Jesus and were filled with the Spirit of God, they did not tremble. The mantle on our life will make us fearless if we choose to walk in it. This is what happened to me. As the Spirit of the Lord would move on me, this power and boldness would arise. I was as amazed as any. It was the mantling of the Lord that changed me from a weak and timid person to one who could stand without fear. This enabled me to not neglect the gift, but to use it. God will break the spirit of fear and cause us operate in the mantle we have received through impartation.

## Laying on Hands

As I have said before, there are at least four different ways to receive an impartation of a mantle. The first one I will mention is through laying on of hands. We see Moses imparting a couple of mantles to Joshua through his hands. One is in Numbers 27:18-20.

> *And the Lord said to Moses: "Take Joshua the son of Nun with you, a man in whom is the Spirit, and lay your hand on him; set him before*

*Eleazar the priest and before all the congrega-*
*tion, and inaugurate him in their sight. And you*
*shall give some of your authority to him, that all*
*the congregation of the children of Israel may be*
*obedient."*

Authority in the spirit world can be given through the laying on of hands. There is a literal transmission of spiritual forces through this activity. This is because laying on of hands is not just symbolic, it is the principle of contact and transference. Something flows from one and into the other. Again, this is what Peter did with the man at the Gate Beautiful in Acts 3. Remember, he declared *"such as I have I give to you."* He then touched him. Moses imparted authority to lead Israel into Joshua's life through the laying on of hands. With this authority, Joshua would see many supernatural things done as well. This is because he received a mantle that granted him authority in the spirit world.

The second place we see Moses imparting mantles is when he gave Joshua wisdom in Deuteronomy 34:9. Perhaps this is the same occurrence. It is possible to receive more than one thing when hands are laid on someone. However it occurred, Joshua was equipped with a mantle of wisdom to give direction as they possessed the land.

*Now Joshua the son of Nun was full of the spirit of wisdom, for Moses had laid his hands on him; so the children of Israel heeded him, and did as the Lord had commanded Moses.*

The wisdom that Joshua walked in to empower Israel to possess the promised land was not a natural wisdom. It was heavenly in nature because he had received an impartation from Moses. When you read the book of Joshua, you see this wisdom at work. It caused Joshua to develop strategy to possess the land. In every city they took, there was a battle plan employed out of this wisdom. Then Joshua knew how to divide the land and territory among the nation. This was all a result of the supernatural mantle of wisdom he carried from Moses. It came through the laying on of hands. We see hands being used to impart mantles for service in Acts 6:3-6. There was a need to administrate the feeding of all the widows in the early church. They found seven people who were able to do this. The apostles laid hands on them and commissioned them.

*"Therefore, brethren, seek out from among you seven men of good reputation, full of the Holy Spirit and wisdom, whom we may appoint over this business; but we will give ourselves continually to prayer and to the ministry of the word."*

*And the saying pleased the whole multitude.*
*And they chose Stephen, a man full of faith and*
*the Holy Spirit, and Philip, Prochorus, Nica-*
*nor, Timon, Parmenas, and Nicolas, a proselyte*
*from Antioch, whom they set before the apos-*
*tles; and when they had prayed, they laid hands*
*on them.*

Notice that before hands were laid on them to impart what was needed for service, these were people hungry for God. They were already full of the Holy Spirit and wisdom. Hands imparting mantles adds to what people so often already carry. This results in new levels of effectiveness and fruitfulness. We have already seen where Timothy had gifts because of hands being laid on them. There are several other places where hands are used to impart mantles, gifting, authority, power, and other spiritual substances. When hands are laid on us, we should be ready to receive. The most powerful person alive can lay hands on someone; however, if they aren't ready, they will receive nothing. There must be a drawing at the time of impartation, very similar to the woman with the issue of blood. Luke 8:43-48 records the classic case where this woman drew the power of God out of Jesus and was healed. Her faith, desperation, hunger, and longing put a demand on what was in Jesus.

*Now a woman, having a flow of blood for twelve years, who had spent all her livelihood on physicians and could not be healed by any, came from behind and touched the border of His garment. And immediately her flow of blood stopped.*

*And Jesus said, "Who touched Me?"*

*When all denied it, Peter and those with him said, "Master, the multitudes throng and press You, and You say, 'Who touched Me?' "*

*But Jesus said, "Somebody touched Me, for I perceived power going out from Me." Now when the woman saw that she was not hidden, she came trembling; and falling down before Him, she declared to Him in the presence of all the people the reason she had touched Him and how she was healed immediately.*

*And He said to her, "Daughter, be of good cheer; your faith has made you well. Go in peace."*

Her faith reached in to who Jesus is and gained her healing. When others *pressed on* Jesus, she *touched* Him. If we aren't careful, we can be just one of the multitude in a mode of religion who gets nothing. But if we are truly hungry for Him and what He carries, when that moment of impartation comes, we will draw the very life and power of God out. Jesus knew when power left Him. This is because the woman in this moment reached out and got her miracle by the anointing that lived in Jesus. If we will, in a like manner, posture ourselves in time of impartation, then through the hands of men and women of God we will receive.

## Words of Declaration

A second way that impartation can occur is through a word of declaration. There can be a spoken word that causes something to go into our spirit that we will carry from that point on. Just to illustrate this, it is said of Jesus that with a word, spiritual things moved. Matthew 8:16 records this.

> *When evening had come, they brought to Him many who were demon-possessed. And He cast out the spirits with a word, and healed all who were sick.*

The demon spirits left people when Jesus commanded them to with a word. This is what the centurion soldier understood concerning Jesus. In Luke 7:6-10, we see Jesus going to this Roman soldier's house and healing his servant. As Jesus arrived at this man's residence, the soldier sent another servant to tell him to please not bother to come in. Just speak the word.

*Then Jesus went with them. And when He was already not far from the house, the centurion sent friends to Him, saying to Him, "Lord, do not trouble Yourself, for I am not worthy that You should enter under my roof. Therefore I did not even think myself worthy to come to You. But say the word, and my servant will be healed. For I also am a man placed under authority, having soldiers under me. And I say to one, 'Go,' and he goes; and to another, 'Come,' and he comes; and to my servant, 'Do this,' and he does it."*

*When Jesus heard these things, He marveled at him, and turned around and said to the crowd that followed Him, "I say to you, I have not found such great faith, not even in Israel!" And those who were sent, returning to the house, found the servant well who had been sick.*

This man knew that the word spoken from the authority of Jesus would cause a healing mantle to enter his house. He had an awareness of how things can operate in the spirit world. He knew Jesus had authority because He walked under the authority of heaven. He understood this because of the authority he carried as one under Roman rule. Just like his authority moved men in the natural, he knew Jesus' authority would move things in the spiritual. If we can get this, a word can impart a mantle to us. A simple word spoken under the authority of the Holy Spirit can impart a mantle that will redirect our lives. Remember that Psalm 107:20 declares that a word can bring healing and deliverance from destruction.

> *He sent His word and healed them,*
> *And delivered them from their destructions.*

This is because the word can carry spiritual forces and even empower with mantles from the Lord. Never diminish the idea of the impartation of a mantle by a simple spoken word under the unction of the Holy Spirit.

## Prophecy

Another way mantles are imparted is through the prophetic. This is similar to a declared word, yet it can be different. Again, Paul told Timothy in First Timothy 4:14 that he had gifts in his life because they were imparted.

> *Do not neglect the gift that is in you, which was*
> *given to you by prophecy with the laying on of*
> *the hands of the eldership.*

Notice that Paul declared that through the mixture of laying on of hands and the prophetic word, gifts were given to Timothy. Spoken prophetic words can impart gifts and mantles into our life. This is because God's Word releases a creative force. As the Lord said to Reinhard Bonnke, *"My word in your mouth is just as powerful as My word in My mouth."* When the Lord allows the prophetic to flow in impartation, it can impart mantles. Hebrews 11:3 tells us that the Word of God creates and brings to order.

> *By faith we understand that the worlds were framed by the word of God, so that the things which are seen were not made of things which are visible.*

This verse doesn't say God made the worlds from nothing. It says He made them of that which we cannot see. The prophetic word of God causes something to come out of the invisible and manifest in the visible. This is why prophecy can be so powerful in impartation of mantles.

This is something that has happened to me many times. Years ago, while I was in training for ministry under an apostolic leader, I had no real ability in the Word of God. I would listen to my apostolic father preach and teach the Word. I was enraptured and longed to be able to bring such revelation. However, there was nothing. As much as I wanted it, I had no ability in the Word of God. I would try to conjure things up, twist it, and make it *revelation*, but there was no inspiration. I remember going into my apostle's office to show him my latest, greatest revelation. I remember it was from Matthew 13. I don't recall what I was saying about it, but I just wanted to be affirmed that I was getting things from the Word. As I began to tell my leader this wonderful truth I had uncovered, he looked at me and said, *"I don't think so, Brother Robert."*

I was devastated. Not because he was being mean, because he wasn't. But because I knew he was right. I literally went and found an isolated place and began to weep. I was broken. How could I be in ministry and fulfill the call of God on my life with no revelation? It looked bleak. However, because we were faithful, not too long afterward we were scheduled to be set in as small group leaders. This didn't require developing teaching, only taking the Sunday morning message and facilitating discussion. Because this was a new thing that was being launched in the church at this time, they were going to pray over all the leaders on a Sunday morning who would lead these groups.

I expressly remember sitting in chairs on the platform. As our apostolic leader began to go from person to person laying his hand on them and commissioning them, he got to me. As he laid his hands on me, he began to prophesy. He declared, *"Robert, the Lord says to you, your life is not your own. You are Mine."* At that instant something happened in my spirit. It was like the hand of God reached on the inside of me and flipped a switch on. Revelation in the Word of God came alive. Whereas I had no insight before, it began now to flow like a river. Until this very day, this gift or mantle still works in me. It was given to me though prophecy. As the Lord declared through my apostolic leader that *"I was His,"* it was as if I was being set apart for service to Him. He gave me a mantle that day of revelation in the Word of God to be able to fulfill that service. It came through the prophetic word of God.

## Atmospheres

The final way that impartation of mantles can come is from *atmosphere*. It is possible to simply receive mantles from being in the right environment. This is why the people we hang out with are so important. The right people create an atmosphere where mantles can come upon us for life and function. As I am consistently in these kinds of atmospheres, the power of God in those places will change my life. We read about the cloud coming down to fellowship with Moses in Exodus 33:8-11. I love this account.

*So it was, whenever Moses went out to the tab-*
*ernacle, that all the people rose, and each man*
*stood at his tent door and watched Moses until*
*he had gone into the tabernacle. And it came to*
*pass, when Moses entered the tabernacle, that the*
*pillar of cloud descended and stood at the door of*
*the tabernacle, and the Lord talked with Moses.*
*All the people saw the pillar of cloud standing at*
*the tabernacle door, and all the people rose and*
*worshiped, each man in his tent door. So the Lord*
*spoke to Moses face to face, as a man speaks to his*
*friend. And he would return to the camp, but his*
*servant Joshua the son of Nun, a young man, did*
*not depart from the tabernacle.*

Notice that Moses would finish communing with
the Lord in this setting. He would go back into the
camp. However, Joshua, who was a young man being
prepared, would stay in the tabernacle before God. He
would allow the presence and glory of that atmosphere
to be imparted to his soul.

How we need people like this today. In my forma-
tive time of training, I would go into the sanctuary by
myself just to seek the Lord. I would spend time in
His presence. I look back now and realize those times
in these atmospheres let me catch the anointing of
God. My being was being fashioned, but mantles and

anointing were also being imparted. We need to treasure these atmospheres. These moments can and will change our life forever. There were other more intense times when I was allowed the opportunity to sit on the platform of a highly anointed ministry. There were time of hands-on impartation. However, just being in the atmosphere for extended times imparted anointing and mantles into my life. I would go to these meetings at great expense and great effort just to be in the atmosphere. The result was that mantles were imparted. I began to see similar things happen in our meetings that happened in these meetings. I had gleaned from the power and glory in these atmospheres. The commandment of God in scripture was to leave the corners of the field to be gleaned by the poor. We see this is Leviticus 19:9-10.

> *When you reap the harvest of your land, you shall not wholly reap the corners of your field, nor shall you gather the gleanings of your harvest. And you shall not glean your vineyard, nor shall you gather every grape of your vineyard; you shall leave them for the poor and the stranger: I am the Lord your God.*

The harvest was for those who had sowed, planted, and harvested it. Yet there was a portion for those who had not labored. They could gather and eat from the field they had not labored to produce. This is what we do when we come into the atmosphere created by others. In this atmosphere of glory and empowerment, great spiritual encounter can occur. I think this is what the Greek woman with the demonized daughter did in Matthew 15:26-28. This woman was crying after the Lord as a Gentile. Jesus at this stage was only sent to the lost sheep of Israel. Yet this woman, through her persistence and faith, got the power of God to her daughter.

> *But He answered and said, "It is not good to take the children's bread and throw it to the little dogs."*
>
> *And she said, "Yes, Lord, yet even the little dogs eat the crumbs which fall from their masters' table."*
>
> *Then Jesus answered and said to her, "O woman, great is your faith! Let it be to you as you desire." And her daughter was healed from that very hour.*

When Jesus referred to her ethnicity as a dog, she was not offended. Desperate people don't get offended. She simply responded by drawing upon rights that she cited. When she spoke of a dog eating the crumbs from the table, I believe she was enacting the gleaning principle. She was saying that even though she was outside the covenant, she should be allowed to eat from the table of the Lord. The Lord was so impressed with her faith and posture that He released the word of healing.

We glean from atmospheres and pull in that which others have labored to produce. Out of the goodness of the Lord, we take hold of the pregnant atmosphere and pull the mantling of God into our lives.

> Lord, as we come before Your Courts, we thank You for the mantles of the Lord. Help us to be diligent to steward these mantles and not neglect them. Forgive us of any pride, arrogance, or wrong motives. I ask for Your blood to speak for us right now and silence any accuser seeking to deny us our mantles from You.
>
> I also ask that I might receive of these mantles through hands being laid on, words declared, prophetic gifting, and atmospheres created. Give me a drawing heart that will not let these pass by. I want the mantle I have been built to carry. I ask that no resistance of the enemy will stand against me and the mantling of God. I receive the impartation of God to move in new levels of power. In Jesus' Name, amen.

# CHAPTER 11

# MANTLES AND TEAM BUILDING

Anything that is successful and culturally impacting will be done through a team. In other words, one person will have limitations on how far they can take a vision or dream. Regardless of whether it's a church, business, institution, or any organization, a multi-personnel entity is required to accomplish the intent. The problem is there must be a people with the same heart, mind, and spirit if this is to be done. I am of the opinion that a big part of this is walking under the same mantle. This is what happened to Moses while leading the children of Israel. Numbers 11:25-29 chronicles the Lord taking the Spirit that was on Moses and placing it on seventy leaders.

> *Then the Lord came down in the cloud, and spoke to him, and took of the Spirit that was upon him, and placed the same upon the seventy elders; and*

*it happened, when the Spirit rested upon them, that they prophesied, although they never did so again.*

*But two men had remained in the camp: the name of one was Eldad, and the name of the other Medad. And the Spirit rested upon them. Now they were among those listed, but who had not gone out to the tabernacle; yet they prophesied in the camp. And a young man ran and told Moses, and said, "Eldad and Medad are prophesying in the camp."*

*So Joshua the son of Nun, Moses' assistant, one of his choice men, answered and said, "Moses my lord, forbid them!"*

*Then Moses said to him, "Are you zealous for my sake? Oh, that all the Lord's people were prophets and that the Lord would put His Spirit upon them!"*

Clearly God mantled these seventy with a portion of the Holy Spirit who was on Moses. This was for the purpose of helping Moses care for the people. The burden of the work and the people was too much for one man to carry. However, it couldn't just be any people who were chosen to do this work. It had to be ones who carried the same heart, mind, and spirit. God accomplished this supernaturally through taking what was on Moses and placing it on these. We see in Numbers 11:16-17 that the purpose was so the burden could be spread across a larger group of people.

> *So the Lord said to Moses: "Gather to Me seventy men of the elders of Israel, whom you know to be the elders of the people and officers over them; bring them to the tabernacle of meeting, that they may stand there with you. Then I will come down and talk with you there. I will take of the Spirit that is upon you and will put the same upon them; and they shall bear the burden of the people with you, that you may not bear it yourself alone."*

When people come under that same mantle, their minds and hearts start to be shaped by that mantle. They are able to walk in agreement to see a job done. I know from experience that when a mantle is received it can alter your personality, behavior, and traits. As I was mantled by a specific ministry, I was amazed that my tendencies started to reflect that minister. I found myself doing things like he did. It wasn't something I thought out or purposed to do. I just found myself doing it that way. I believe it is because I received of the mantle that he carried. People thought that I was trying to imitate this person. It wasn't so. The mantle I received began to shape my thoughts, activities, and even personality to some extent. This doesn't mean we become little imitations of someone else. However, it does mean that we can began to think a certain way so that can occur. This is what Paul said about Titus, his son in the faith. In Second Corinthians 12:18 we see Paul speaking of Titus and how he behaved himself among the Corinthians.

> *I urged Titus, and sent our brother with him. Did Titus take advantage of you? Did we not walk in the same spirit? Did we not walk in the same steps?*

Titus and Paul were of the same spirit. They walked in the same steps. This wasn't because Paul told Titus to be like him. It was because as a son, Titus carried the same mantling as Paul. This allowed this consistency between the two. People who don't understand this can accuse the leader of being a controller. They can think that they are making people do something a certain way. However, often it is caused by the spirit that has been received and the mantle that actually carried the personality of the leader. It is very apparent that when Elisha asked for the mantle/anointing from Elijah it was the spirit of Elijah that was requested. Just one more time let's see this scripture in Second Kings 2:9.

*And so it was, when they had crossed over, that Elijah said to Elisha, "Ask! What may I do for you, before I am taken away from you?"*

*Elisha said, "Please let a double portion of your spirit be upon me."*

Notice it was a double portion of *your spirit* that was requested. Obviously it was the power of the Holy Spirit that came on him, but it was also the spirit of Elijah. Elisha receive not only the powerful anointing of God. He also received the spirit of Elijah, which would have involved his nature and even mannerisms. This would have allowed him to walk in a certain way by nature.

This is absolutely essential for a team operation. Each person will carry their own gifting. However, the way they think and operate comes into a consistency when mantles are received. We are told in Amos 3:3 that there must be agreement for people to walk together.

*Can two walk together, unless they are agreed?*

The agreement of people together can be greatly accelerated when the mantle of the leader is imparted to the individual team members. This doesn't mean people become robots or without choices in matters. It means there is a certain spirit that is among the team. It isn't hard or difficult to now function in a certain way, because the mantle has changed the way I see things. This is why Jesus said that when people saw Him they saw the Father. They walked in the same Spirit. John 14:9 depicts this thought.

> *Jesus said to him, "Have I been with you so long, and yet you have not known Me, Philip? He who has seen Me has seen the Father; so how can you say, 'Show us the Father'?"*

Jesus as the Son displayed the very heart and nature of the Father. We know on a bigger scale this is about Jesus being God. However, it unveils this principle that sons manifest fathers. This is because through relationship and fellowship the mantle of the father has come on the son. This is why Titus and Paul walked in the same spirit. Titus, as I said, was a son to Paul. Titus 1:4 declares this expressly.

> *To Titus, a true son in our common faith: Grace, mercy, and peace from God the Father and the Lord Jesus Christ our Savior.*

This is what allowed Titus to so reflect Paul and the mantle he carried. Mantles shape the way we think and see things. This is imperative for a team to operate. Without the impartation of mantles as happened with

Moses and the seventy, this team connection may take years, or it may never happen at all.

It is interesting that those who came out with Moses received the impartation of the Spirit. Yet there were two left in the camp who didn't come out for whatever reason. They also received. Clearly they were numbered among the ones chosen to carry this Spirit. I think also that the reason the two who didn't come out with the rest received was because of the heart they had. They were appointed and chosen of God because they were of the prepared of God. Their names reveal who these two were. Eldad means *God has loved*. Medad means *affectionate, loving*. These two had a heart of love for God and the people. Therefore, God chose them though they weren't among those who had come out to meet with Moses. This offended Joshua. However, Moses was wise enough to know that if the Holy Spirit was mantling them, then they should be acknowledged.

When you want to know who God is choosing, then just look at who He is mantling. Very rarely will we go wrong in choosing team members from this criteria. The Holy Spirit fell on Eldad and Medad because their love for God and the people would allow them to minister effectively. They would be able to help meet the needs once mantled with the Spirit that was on Moses. Joshua was offended because he had spent much time with Moses in the presence of the Lord. Here God was allowing His Spirit to fall on these who seemingly hadn't done so. Moses' response was that God desired all His people to be prophets and be under this Spirit. In other words, God is not stingy with the Holy Spirit. Whoever is hungry and prepared of the Lord, God will allow His Spirit to empower them. There are certain principles that attract the anointing and mantling of the Lord. However, there are times when God just sovereignly decides to do something. It is His choice whom He anoints, and we must simply agree with it and surrender to it. It may not be what we think should be done, but God is God.

Many people come with their own agendas. I have seen it through the years when building and leading a team. However, if they can come under the mantle of the leader, this can be greatly alleviated. People can become of one spirit, heart, and mind because of the effect of the mantle over their lives. Here is a prayer that we might use to impart the mantle to our team members.

> Lord, as we come into the Courts of Heaven, I bring this ministry that I lead. Lord, may this entity have a book in heaven. May it have a divine purpose and reason for existence. Lord, You have set me as leader over

this entity and its team. I believe You have anointed me to lead this team and fulfill Your will in the earth through this. I now ask that the mantle You have placed on me might be imparted to each team member. Let the anointing of the Holy Spirit now come on each of us chosen by You to be a part of this team. Let us walk in the same heart, mind, and spirit with one agenda and purpose. I release Your mantle for this now from the Courts of Heaven, In Jesus' Name. Amen.

# CHAPTER 12

# MANTLED WITH GRACE

In a previous chapter, we saw that grace is imparted to us when we receive a mantle from the Lord. In concluding this book, I want to talk about the mantles that carry many different facets of the grace of God. When I think of First Peter 4:10 and the *manifold* grace of God, it directs my mind in a certain way.

> *As each one has received a gift, minister it to one another, as good stewards of the manifold grace of God.*

Remember that the *manifold* grace of God speaks of many different aspects of the grace of God. Different giftings, different propensities, different anointings result from the kind of grace we have received. Joseph in Genesis 37:3-4 was given a coat of many colors by his father. This is a picture to me of the manifold grace of God coming on him.

*Now Israel loved Joseph more than all his chil-
dren, because he was the son of his old age. Also
he made him a tunic of many colors. But when
his brothers saw that their father loved him more
than all his brothers, they hated him and could
not speak peaceably to him.*

I am not suggesting that favoritism should be shown
in the home. However, Israel/Jacob loved Joseph in a
special way. If you will, he mantled Joseph with this
tunic of many colors. This was not just a beautiful coat.
It was a prophetic declaration of the multi-natured
grace of God that Joseph would walk in. He would be a
highly gifted man who would be used to save nations.
The Bible says in Genesis 45:5 that God sent Joseph
ahead to preserve life.

*But now, do not therefore be grieved or angry
with yourselves because you sold me here; for
God sent me before you to preserve life.*

When Israel/Jacob mantled Joseph with this coat,
even though he didn't know it, he was mantling him
with "grace for grace" to be this preserver of life. This
is a term used in John 1:16 to describe the manifold
grace of God.

*And of His fullness we have all received, and
grace for grace.*

Jacob/Israel is a picture of the heavenly Father in this account. The heavenly Father's love for us compels Him to mantle us with a coat/mantle for our destiny and future. This mantle that Joseph carried declared and depicted the Father's love over his life. So mantles do for us as well. When the Father mantles us, it is something we will carry that speaks that we are special to God. People who are insecure in their own relationship with the Father will potentially have trouble with this.

This is what happened with Joseph's brothers. They detested him because of the love and favor of their father over him. It even caused them to do the unthinkable. When Joseph approached his brothers on an assignment from his father, they took him and stripped him of his coat. Genesis 37:23 shows this is the first thing they did to him before they sold him into slavery.

> *So it came to pass, when Joseph had come to his brothers, that they stripped Joseph of his tunic, the tunic of many colors that was on him.*

We know that they ended up selling him into slavery and concocting an elaborate tale that he had been eaten and devoured by a beast. Beasts speak of demons in scripture quite often. So often God's people, the brothers, do devastating things to others and then claim the demons did it.

I think it is interesting that the first thing they did was strip him of the coat that depicted their father's love and favor. They removed the mantle from him. They then dipped it in the blood of a kid or baby goat. They took it to their father and convinced him that Joseph had been killed and devoured by a wild beast. The bottom line is they removed the coat of grace from his life that the father had given him. We cannot allow the criticism and negativity of others to strip from us the awareness of God's love. When Joseph wore this coat, I'm sure it spoke to him of how much his father cared for him. It set him apart from others because of the love his father had for him. The insecure and hateful brothers desired to strip this off him. Yet what Joseph *wore* in the Spirit realm would propel him into his destiny and call as a preserver of life.

We must wear the mantle of grace that empowers us in many different areas. As a result of the mantles of manifold grace on his life, Joseph was used in many areas. What his father had placed on him with this prophetic gift of his coat would serve him and his life. From this mantling, Joseph would administrate the house of Potiphar, lead life in prison, interpret dreams, be promoted from prisoner to prime minister, deal skillfully with the brothers who wronged him, but mostly he would forgive. Those who had done him great wrong were forgiven by Joseph expressly.

After Joseph had brought his family to Egypt to save them from the famine, their father died. His brothers thought that Joseph had been restraining himself until his father was gone; then he would revenge himself on his brothers. Their fear of this caused them to appeal to Joseph. Joseph's response was a depiction of the grace on his life that he had been mantled with. Genesis 50:18-21 tells a little of this story.

> *Then his brothers also went and fell down before his face, and they said, "Behold, we are your servants."*
>
> *Joseph said to them, "Do not be afraid, for am I in the place of God? But as for you, you meant evil against me; but God meant it for good, in order to bring it about as it is this day, to save many people alive. Now therefore, do not be afraid; I will provide for you and your little ones." And he comforted them and spoke kindly to them.*

The brothers appealed to Joseph to please be forgiving toward them. Joseph's response is revealing. When he said, *"Am I in the place of God?"* he was saying that what would happen to them was between them and God. He said that he realized as painful as the process was, and as wrong as they were, God used it. Even though they meant to destroy him, God redeemed it and brought much good out of it. Joseph was not interested in paying them back. In fact, he was interested in providing for them. This was a result of the mantle of multifaceted grace being on his life.

The mantles do not just empower us; they change us to be like Jesus. It is impossible to carry mantles from the Lord and not be changed into His image and likeness. No matter how powerful the mantles of God may be on our life, they will soften us and reveal Jesus in us. This is what happened to Joseph from the mantling of his father. This is what will happen to us as well.

> Lord, as we stand before Your Courts, we ask that we might receive the manifold grace of God from You our Father, as Joseph received the coat from his father. Lord, help us to deal with any backlash from brothers as a result of the mantles we carry from our Father. Let this mantling of grace produce in us the very nature of Jesus as it empowers us to our function and destiny. May we be as Joseph who was a preserver of life. He was used by You to save many from destruction. May this be for us as well. Thank You, Lord, for Your mantling of grace and coat of many colors from our Father. In Jesus' Name. Amen.

# CHAPTER 13

# TAILORED TO FIT THE MANTLE

P art of the dream that launched the whole impartation of mantles showed that I was dressed as a tailor and had a measuring tape in my hand. The word was that I and the tailors with me would be used to fit people into their mantles. This is very profound. My own personal belief is that the mantles are not altered to fit us, but we are altered to fit the mantles. When you take clothes to a tailor, they measure you then do alterations on the garment to fit you. In the spirit realm, however, God uses His tailors to do alterations on us to fit the mantles we are to carry. These tailors are the fivefold ministry gifts that God uses to change us and grow us up. Ephesians 4:11-13 shows that these gifts of men and women to the church are used to bring us into the full measure of who Jesus is.

*And He Himself gave some to be apostles, some prophets, some evangelists, and some pastors and teachers, for the equipping of the saints for the work of ministry, for the edifying of the body of Christ, till we all come to the unity of the faith and of the knowledge of the Son of God, to a perfect man, to the measure of the stature of the fullness of Christ.*

To come to any measurement, you have to be measured. There are times when heaven measures us. This can be scary. For instance, heaven measured Belshazzar, who was the king in Daniel's day in captivity. This king defiled the vessels that had come from the house of the Lord in Jerusalem. This greatly displeased God. If you remember, a hand appeared on the wall and wrote words that couldn't be understood. They called for Daniel to interpret them. Daniel 5:24-28 shows Daniel interpreting that which was written.

*Then the fingers of the hand were sent from Him, and this writing was written.*

*"And this is the inscription that was written:*

*MENE, MENE, TEKEL, UPHARSIN*

*This is the interpretation of each word. MENE: God has numbered your kingdom, and finished it; TEKEL: You have been weighed in the balances,*

*and found wanting; PERES: Your kingdom*
*has been divided, and given to the Medes and*
*Persians."*

Because of his disregard for the Lord, this king was
weighed in the balance. In other words, he was measured. I am citing this to let us know that heaven will
measure us. Of course, we are not afraid of this kind of
judgment, yet we are measured and prepared for the
mantling of the Lord. The Lord will use His servants,
the fivefold ministry gifts, to tailor us to fit the mantles
we are to carry. These gifts will heal us, prepare us,
remove from us, and put into us what we need to carry
the mantles of God. In Revelation 11:1, during John's
encounter in heaven, he was apostolically allowed to
measure and evaluate things.

*Then I was given a reed like a measuring rod.*
*And the angel stood, saying, "Rise and measure*
*the temple of God, the altar, and those who wor-*
*ship there."*

Notice that John measured the temple of God, the
altar, and the worshipers. Apostles are allowed to
measure the house of God or the corporate people of
God. They are allowed to evaluate by the Spirit of God
what is lacking and what is needed. They don't do this
from a critical standpoint, but from an awareness of

what is necessary to fulfill the purposes of God. John also measured the altar or the place of sacrifice and giving. How and what people give is a right thing to be measured. This might shock some but only if they are bound by a spirit of religion. God is always looking at how we give. Jesus did this in Mark 12:41-44.

> *Now Jesus sat opposite the treasury and saw how the people put money into the treasury. And many who were rich put in much. Then one poor widow came and threw in two mites, which make a quadrans. So He called His disciples to Himself and said to them, "Assuredly, I say to you that this poor widow has put in more than all those who have given to the treasury; for they all put in out of their abundance, but she out of her poverty put in all that she had, her whole livelihood."*

Notice that Jesus sat and watched *how* the people gave. He was also aware of *what or how much* because He saw how the rich gave. The bottom line was He was measuring their giving. It was being evaluated by the Son of God. Everything is measured as we prepare to be mantled.

John then measured the worshiper with the measuring reed he was given. Did you know God measures our worship? I remember I had a dream where I was standing before a judge. Obviously, this is speaking of

God the Judge. One of the things brought up in consideration of the judgment that would be passed was my worship. I've always been a worshiper. I love the presence of the Lord and the worship that attracts it. As I've traveled, I've been in many worship settings. Quite honestly, in my opinion, most are empty of the life of God. I would find it very difficult to endure the longevity of most of them. I would sense no real presence of the Lord. After much of this, I just endured it and stopped *worshiping.* I would stand or sometimes sit to just get through it all. Then I would go preach and minister after the "singing" was over.

In my dream, I was being measured and judged for *not worshiping.* I was aware that God knew I was checked out during the *worship time.* I had to repent. The truth is that regardless of what is going on, if I am a worshiper, I will worship. It doesn't matter whether I like the style, the music, or the length. I am to worship. Heaven is measuring it and apostles are called to use the measuring rod form heaven to measure with.

It is interesting that John didn't measure with something he had. He measured with what the angel gave him. As apostles, we are to measure out of the measurement of heaven. Most of the time we measure from earth. We measure based on someone else's life. This is what we are warned against in Second Corinthians 10:12. We are not measure our life by someone else's.

*For we dare not class ourselves or compare ourselves with those who commend themselves. But they, measuring themselves by themselves, and comparing themselves among themselves, are not wise.*

This measurement will not accomplish what God wants. We are not to be measured by and then tailored to earthly standards. We are to be measured by the measuring rod of God in the hands of the fivefold ministry. When this happens, we are not unwise but walking in the wisdom of God.

It is the Word of God that measures us. Second Timothy 3:16-17 tells us the measuring and revealing nature of the Word.

*All Scripture is given by inspiration of God, and is profitable for doctrine, for reproof, for correction, for instruction in righteousness, that the man of God may be complete, thoroughly equipped for every good work.*

Notice that the Word reproves, corrects, and instructs us. This speaks that it is measuring us and causing us to change. This process will result in us being tailored to fit the mantle God has for us. The Word is a mirror that reflects back to us who we really are. I can think I'm awesome until I look into the mirror. The mirror doesn't lie. It reflects back to us who we really are. James 1:23-25 lets us know that as we look at ourselves in the mirror of His Word, we have to change what isn't measuring up.

> *For if anyone is a hearer of the word and not a doer, he is like a man observing his natural face in a mirror; for he observes himself, goes away, and immediately forgets what kind of man he was. But he who looks into the perfect law of liberty and continues in it, and is not a forgetful hearer but a doer of the work, this one will be blessed in what he does.*

We become blessed in our life because we are lining ourselves up with the mirror of His Word. This is why we must read the Word, study the Word, feed on the Word, but also sit under the Word from the fivefold ministry gifts. Their job is not to entertain us; it is to bring us into the full measure of the stature of Christ. They are to minister the life of God from under the anointing until we are changed to fit the mantle of God. As we do this, heaven is recording this and releasing judgments in our favor. We will be tailored and fitted for the mantle of God from heaven.

Lord, as I come before Your Courts, I allow the tailoring of God through the fivefold ministry gifts into my life. Let me be measured and shaped by the Word of God. Thank You, Lord, for Your measuring for my life. Use Your gifts to tailor me. Let me be tailored to fit the mantle that has been assigned to me. Let me be tailored as a part of the house of God. Let me be measured and tailored in my giving and sacrifice. Let my worship be acceptable to You in Spirit and in Truth. Lord, let these things be recorded in Jesus' Name in Your Courts, O God.

Now, Lord, let the mantle of God flow into my life. Let all that has been assigned me from the mantle closet of God now be imparted into my life. I receive Your mantle from the Courts of Heaven. Thank You so much for this precious gift, In Jesus' Name. Amen.

# ABOUT
# ROBERT HENDERSON

Robert Henderson is a global apostolic leader who operates in revelation and impartation. His teaching empowers the body of Christ to see the hidden truths of scripture clearly and apply them for breakthrough results. Driven by a mandate to disciple nations through writing and speaking, Robert travels extensively around the globe, teaching on the apostolic, the Kingdom of God, the "Seven Mountains," and, most notably, the Courts of Heaven. He has been married to Mary for 40 years. They have six children and five grandchildren. Together they are enjoying life in beautiful Waco, Texas.

# INCREASE THE EFFECTIVENESS OF YOUR PRAYERS.

*Learn how to release your destiny from Heaven's Courts!*

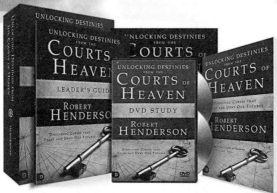

## Unlocking Destinies from the Courts of Heaven

*Curriculum Box Set Includes:*
*9 Video Teaching Sessions (2 DVD Disks),* Unlocking Destinies *book,*
*Interactive Manual, Leader's Guide*

There are books in Heaven that record your destiny and purpose. Their pages describe the very reason you were placed on the Earth.

And yet, there is a war against your destiny being fulfilled. Your archenemy, the devil, knows that as you occupy your divine assignment, by default, the powers of darkness are demolished. Heaven comes to Earth as God's people fulfill their Kingdom callings!

In the *Unlocking Destinies from the Courts of Heaven* book and curriculum, Robert Henderson takes you step by step through a prophetic prayer strategy. By watching the powerful video sessions and going through the Courts of Heaven process using the interactive manual, you will learn how to dissolve the delays and hindrances to your destiny being fulfilled.

# YOUR Prophetic COMMUNITY

## Are you passionate about hearing God's voice, walking with Jesus, and experiencing the power of the Holy Spirit?

Destiny Image is a community of believers with a passion for equipping and encouraging you to live the prophetic, supernatural life you were created for!

We offer a fresh helping of practical articles, dynamic podcasts, and powerful videos from respected, Spirit-empowered, Christian leaders to fuel the holy fire within you.

### Sign up now to get awesome content delivered to your inbox
### destinyimage.com/sign-up

 Destiny Image